T·H·E   C·O·M·P·L·E·T·E
H·O·M·E
C·O·N·F·E·C·T·I·O·N·E·R

Hilary Walden

T·H·E C·O·M·P·L·E·T·E

H·O·M·E
C·O·N·F·E·C·T·I·O·N·E·R

Hilary Walden

CHARTWELL
BOOKS, INC.

A QUARTO BOOK

Published by Chartwell Books Inc
A Division of Book Sales Inc,
110 Enterprise Avenue
Secausus, New Jersey 07094

ISBN 1 55521 138 0
This book was designed and produced by
Quarto Publishing Limited
The Old Brewery
6 Blundell Street
London N7 9BH

Senior Editor Lorraine Dickey
Editors Barbara Croxford, Lisa Hardy
Art Editor Moira Clinch
Design Assistant Vincent Murphy
Photography Paul Forrester
Home Economist Philippa Caney

Art Director Alastair Campbell
Editorial Director Carolyn King

Equipment courtesy of David Mellor, 26 James Street, Covent Garden;
4 Sloane Square; 66 King Street, Manchester.
China courtesy of The General Store, Covent Garden.
Gas Hob courtesy of Wiles Ltd.
Border illustration on pages 46, 47 designed by Collier Campbell.
Border illustration on pages 52, 53 designed by Ann Brecknell, Gordon
Fraser Gallery Ltd.

Filmset by Text Filmsetters Limited, London SE1

Manufactured in Hong Kong by Regent Publishing Services Limited
Printed by Lee Fung Asco Printers Ltd, Hong Kong

C·O·N·T·E·N·T·S

I·N·T·R·O·D·U·C·T·I·O·N

Making candies is therapeutic, rewarding and fun, and does not require complicated, costly equipment or ingredients that are difficult to obtain. Homemade candies are less expensive than their mass-produced commercial counterparts, are guaranteed free from preservatives and artificial additives, and have the true taste of the traditional, old-fashioned favorites, a taste that is all too frequently missing from the store-bought versions.

The idea of making candies can, at first, seem daunting, but the practice itself is straightforward and the necessary know-how easy to acquire. Don't be put off either if, on the first read, candy recipes seem complicated. They're not. They consist of a number of basic techniques that are easy to master if they are taken step by step, especially if the steps are both illustrated and explained, as in this book. Practice, too, is important, so don't be surprised to find that it takes you a couple of trial runs to get your technique right. Use family or close friends as guinea-pigs for your first attempts before you consider making large batches to solve all your gift problems at Christmas or birthdays or filling a homemade candy stall at a local fête. Start with the simplest candies to gain experience and confidence before attempting the more complicated ones – for example, it is best to try your hand at barley sugar sticks before tackling humbugs, and from there you can move on to simple 'pulled' candy cushions.

Candy making can't be rushed, so always allow plenty of time – it can take a surprisingly long time for 2 cups of sugar to melt. Avoid, too, making candies on damp days or in a damp atmosphere, such as a steamy kitchen.

Homemade candies are ideal for giving as gifts with that truly personal touch, and are satisfying to both receiver and giver alike. There are so many different types – sophisticated, sinful truffles and

humbugs, playful sugar mice, conversation-stopping toffees, refreshing fruit jellies, melting fudge, to name but a few – and they can be wrapped and presented in so many different ways. With homemade candies you will never be at a loss as to what to give to anyone, no matter what their age or taste.

Children are usually very interested in seeing how their treats are made and there are various recipes for simple candies and uncooked versions of the 'classics', such as fondant, that they can have fun helping with or making on their own. Wrapping up the candies too is a job for which their small, nimble fingers are often well suited. But remember never to leave a child unsupervised when sugar syrups are being made as they can cause nasty burns.

Sugar is a prerequisite of all candies, but there are so many different forms and types of sugar that can be used in candy making that the fundamental sweetness need never become boring or monotonous. Instead, it can be full of surprises – the dark sweetness with a back-note of sharpness from black treacle or molasses, the fresh tang of fruit sugar, the warmth of brown sugar or the clarity of superfine sugar. Further variety and interest is given by all the other ingredients that can be incorporated with the sugar, from the smooth, luxurious richness of cream and butter, the crunch of nuts, the characteristic taste of chocolate to the lightness of stiffly beaten egg whites.

Candy making has the reputation for being a very skilled branch of cookery, one to be left to the professional confectioner. This is true to some extent but, with very few particularly specialist exceptions, none is beyond the scope of a careful, precise cook and some are child's play, quite literally.

Candy making requires only a little practice and attention to simple details. You will find in the following sections all the information and technical advice necessary for success in this immensely satisfying and creative branch of the culinary arts.

B·A·S·I·C
M·E·T·H·O·D·S

E·Q·U·I·P·M·E·N·T

The basic equipment needed for making candies is minimal. Indeed to make some, no more is required than a bowl or work surface, and most can be made using equipment that is found in the majority of kitchens. For other items such as dipping forks and fondant mats, pay a visit to a good hardware store, department store or kitchen-ware store.

• SAUCEPANS •

Good quality, heavy, deep saucepans are most important. Those made from cast-iron, copper, aluminum or stainless steel are most suitable for the high temperatures that are reached when making sugar syrups. In a thin saucepan the syrup will heat unevenly and will 'catch' and burn easily.

As the syrup will rise in the pan as it boils, choose a saucepan that has a capacity about four times as great as the amount of ingredients being used, and choose a deep one rather than a wide shallow one.

The best way to clean a saucepan after it has been used for candy making is to fill it immediately with hot water and leave it to simmer, covered, until the syrup has dissolved.

• CANDY THERMOMETER •

A special thermometer that will withstand the temperature of a boiling, concentrated syrup makes successful candy making much easier.

The graduations should be easy to read and should be calibrated from 60°F to 360°F, usually with markings to indicate the various stages of the sugar-boiling process and with some form of clip for fixing the thermometer to the side of the saucepan. To 'season' a new thermometer, place it in a saucepan of cold water, heat the water gently to boiling point, then leave the thermometer to cool in the water. Before starting to make a syrup, place the thermometer in fairly hot water to warm it up. Otherwise, if put straight into a hot syrup, it might crack.

When using the thermometer in a syrup, make sure that it is standing upright, that the bulb is completely covered but is not touching the bottom of the pan, and that no sugar crystals accumulate around the bulb. Take the reading at eye-level.

• PANS •

For 'homely' candies where a perfect appearance is unnecessary, any heatproof container will do – such as a casserole dish, ice-cube tray with the divider removed or aluminum foil dishes, but for more 'serious' candy making, it's best to use cake pans. Ordinary square or rectangular straight-sided ones are quite adequate, with 6-8 inch square ones being the most useful, although obviously the size varies with the amount being made. However, the exact size of pan is not absolutely vital as a change in the dimensions will simply mean thicker or thinner candies.

Pans have to be prepared before being filled with the candy mixture, but the type of preparation is governed by the type of candy being made. Pans for jellies should be sprinkled with cold water, those for Turkish delight sprinkled with an even coating of cornstarch mixed with sugar. If the candies are turned out of the pan before cutting, the pan is lined with, in the instance of nougat, rice paper.

A non-stick coating on a pan is an advantage in all candy making.

• SPATULAS AND METAL SPATULAS •

A wooden spatula is the easiest equipment to use for working fondants, but flexible metal spatulas are more suitable for turning toffee mixtures and spreading pralines.

• WORK SURFACES •

The traditional, professional surface is marble, but any heat-absorbent, smooth surface will do – a large baking sheet or a well-oiled heavy wooden chopping board, for example.

Avoid pouring very hot syrups on to laminated surfaces which are not able to withstand high temperatures.

• SPATULAS AND PALETTE KNIVES •

A wooden spatula is the easiest equipment to use for working fondants, but flexible metal palette knives are more suitable for turning toffee mixtures and spreading pralines.

1 Good quality, heavy, deep saucepan

2 A selection of baking pans

3 A glass heatproof bowl

4 A selection of aspic cutters

5 A pair of heavy-duty, sharp kitchen scissors

6 A selection of fondant cutters

7 A fondant mat

8 A molded tray for shaped fondants and chocolates

9 A wooden spatula

10 A wooden spoon

11 A small metal spatula

12 A large metal spatula

13 A candy thermometer

14 A pronged dipping fork

15 A circular dipping fork

16 A marble slab

•CONTAINERS AND WRAPPINGS•

*1 A selection of colored tissue
paper paper and foil
2 Rolls of colored cellophane
paper
3 Cardboard leaf and flower
shapes*

*4 Paper candy cases
5 Small flower-shaped dishes
6 Different sizes of clear glass
jars with ground glass tops
7 A selection of wrapped
candies*

• SCISSORS •

Strong, sharp kitchen scissors are needed for cutting toffees and pulled candies.

• METAL CUTTERS •

A selection of shapes and sizes of sharp metal cutters are required for marshmallows, fondants and marzipans.

• DIPPING FORKS •

Dipping forks can either have a loop at one end or two or three prongs. In addition to being used for dipping candies they can be used to mark the surface with a pattern or design, but are not vital for either task; carving forks, fondue forks or ordinary kitchen forks can easily be used instead.

• FONDANT MAT •

A fondant mat is rather like a rubber ice-cube tray except that the indentations are a selection of decorative shapes. They can be used for shaping creams and chocolates as well as fondants.

• WRAPPING MATERIALS •

A number of materials can be used for wrapping candies individually. The most straightforward is waxed paper but, for a more attractive presentation, clear cellophane or plastic wrap can be used to show off the gloss and shiny color of candies to full effect. Aluminum foil and metallic wrapping paper, available in a wide range of colors from stationers and gift stores, can be very attractive. Alternatively, colored cellophane can be used.

The wrapping for square or oblong candies can either be folded over neatly to make a tidy parcel or it can simply be folded over the candies and two opposite ends twisted in opposite directions. This method is most suitable for round candies, humbugs or cushions.

Candies that are not wrapped can be put in small plain paper candy cases or into pretty decorated or foil ones. If two layers of candies rather than a single one are packed inside a box, separate the layers with a sheet of waxed paper.

• STORAGE CONTAINERS AND STORING •

Unless candies are to be eaten very soon after they have been made, they should be protected from the moisture in the atmosphere to prevent them becoming sticky. Some candies such as caramels, toffees, boiled and 'pulled' candies, must be wrapped individually before being placed in containers, while others, such as marshmallows, can simply be put carefully into a container that has first been lined with waxed paper.

Containers may be made of any material provided it is airtight and inert (with no smell that would taint the candies). Glass jars allow the natural sparkle and color of candies or colorful wrappings to be displayed invitingly. If the jar does not have a suitable lid, cover it tightly with foil, cellophane or plastic wrap, and secure it firmly with string or sticky tape.

Store all candies in a cool, dry place. In general, the harder the candy, the longer it will keep.

• A GUIDE TO STORAGE TIMES •

Simple candies	Eat quickly as their perishable contents tend to dry out
Truffles	2-3 days
Chocolates	10-14 days
Jellies	2 weeks
Nutty Candies	2 weeks
Candied and crystallized fruits	6 months
Fudge	3-4 weeks
Caramels	10-14 days
Marzipan, uncooked	1-2 days
Marzipan, unshaped but cooked	3-4 weeks
Marzipan candies	Eat within 3 weeks
Boiled candies	3-4 weeks
Nougat	3-4 weeks
Toffees	2 weeks
Fondant, uncooked	Use immediately
Fondant, boiled	6 months

I·N·G·R·E·D·I·E·N·T·S

The ingredients list for most candies are very short and simple, and all the important ingredients are in everyday use or readily available. Even the more specialist ingredients, such as concentrated food flavors or glucose, are not too difficult to obtain as they are stocked by good food stores or drugstores.

• SUGAR •

Sugar is synonymous with candies, and its many forms and states can be used to produce different types of candies, with each type of sugar imparting different characteristics to the candy.

Granulated. This is suitable for most recipes that are heated, but its large crystals will give a rather granular texture to uncooked confections.

Caster. This has finer crystals, therefore dissolves more readily. Thus it is more suitable than granulated for uncooked pastes.

Confectioners'. This has a very fine texture so is ideal for uncooked candies that must be very smooth. It is also sprinkled onto the work surface and rolling pin to prevent mixtures sticking when they are rolled out, and it is sprinkled into pans, when making marshmallows, for example.

Light soft brown. Fine grained with moist, clinging crystals that dissolve easily and impart a mild, yet distinctive flavor, this sugar is often used for fudge.

Dark soft brown. This sugar is richly flavored and colored, with moist, fine crystals that tend to clump together yet dissolve readily.

Brown granulated. This has a rich flavor with light golden crystals that remain separate but, as they are large, melt slowly. Because of this, it is best used in mixtures that are boiled to a high temperature, such as toffee.

Glucose. Available in both powder and liquid form, it is added to candy mixtures to help control crystallization. It helps to keep candies made from uncooked fondant soft for longer periods.

Honey. Added for the characteristic flavor it will impart, honey also helps to control crystallization.

Golden syrup. A British product that is a clear, pale, yellow-gold color with a thick, honey-like consistency and mild flavor. Its inclusion in a recipe will help to control crystallization of the sugar.

Corn syrup. An American product with a mild flavor that, like honey and golden syrup, helps to keep the mixture smooth by controlling the formation of sugar crystals.

Black treacle. A thick, dark, richly-flavored syrup that adds distinction to any candy in which it is used. used.

Molasses. This has many similarities to black treacle but is less sweet.

• BUTTER •

Only use good quality unsalted butters, and dice them before use to speed up the melting.

• CHOCOLATE •

Special 'dipping' chocolate or good quality dessert chocolate are the best types to buy for making candies; using cheap 'cooking' chocolate is a waste of your efforts and produces an inferior candy. For that real rich flavor, use a bitter variety of semisweet chocolate.

• MILKS •

Evaporated and condensed milks give more richly flavored candies as they have been subjected to high temperatures for quite long periods during their processing, and so already have a caramel flavor.

• FLAVORINGS •

So that they will not dilute the syrup, any flavorings that are added must be concentrated and sufficiently strong that only a few drops will be enough to flavor a thick candy mixture. They are invariably added at the end of the cooking to avoid loss of strength.

• COLORINGS •

Pure vegetable food colorings are available from good food stores in a wide range of colors. Like flavorings, they are concentrated and used in small amounts.

• INGREDIENTS •

1 Liquid glucose
2 Clear honey
3 Light corn syrup
4 Dark corn syrup
5 Dark, soft brown sugar
6 Light, soft brown sugar
7 Brown sugar
8 Confectioners' sugar
9 Powdered glucose
10 White Sugar
11 Liquid food colorings
12 Semisweet chocolate

A·L·L A·B·O·U·T S·U·G·A·R

Boiling sugar in water to make a syrup is the cornerstone of candy making. and the degree to which the syrup is boiled, or the temperature that it reaches, will determine the type of candy that is made. The more sugar there is in a syrup, or the less water, the higher the temperature of the boiling point of the solution. As the syrup continues to boil, more water evaporates, concentrating the syrup further and raising the boiling point. The greater the sugar content of a syrup, the firmer or harder it will set as it cools: for instance, the syrup for making toffees is taken to a higher temperature than that for making fudge, so the proportion of water is less, and the candy

During the heating the sugar is constantly changing. These changes are related to the temperature and concentration of the syrup, so it is very easy to tell what stage has been reached, either by measuring the temperature or carrying out a simple 'water test' (see page 18).

The initial proportions of water and sugar are not critical as it is the final concentration that matters, but obviously if too much water is added at the start it will take longer to evaporate off the excess and to reach the required temperature, so wasting time and fuel. As the temperature increases, so does the amount of sugar that water will 'take'.

When the syrup cools the sucrose in the sugar in such a syrup is very likely to re-form into crystals unless preventive steps are taken (see below, and individual recipes). But in some sweets this inclination of sugar to crystallize is put to good use – in a *controlled* way – as in the beating of fudges or fondants.

• ANTI-CRYSTALLIZING AGENTS •

Acids such as cream of tartar, lemon juice or vinegar break sucrose down into other sugars.

Sugars other than sucrose could be used, such as honey, liquid glucose or corn syrup.

Milks, cream and butter will thicken the syrup, and so hinder the formation of crystals.

• PREPARING A SUGAR SYRUP •

1 If a candy thermometer is being used, place it in hot water.

2 Measure the sugar and liquid into a clean, thick, deep saucepan that has a capacity of about four times the volume of the ingredients.

3 Heat gently, stirring with a wooden spoon, until the sugar has dissolved.

4 Bring the syrup to a boil without stirring – this would cause crystals to form.

5 Cover the saucepan with a tight-fitting lid so that the steam that condenses on the sides of the pan will wash down any sugar that has crystallized there.

6 An alternative method of removing sugar crystals that form on the side of a saucepan is to use a clean brush dipped in hot water.

7 Remove the lid after about 3 minutes and put the warmed thermometer in position. Leave the syrup to boil until the correct temperature has been reached, adjusting the heat to maintain a steady boil.

If using a testing method (see page 18) rather than a thermometer to check the temperature of the syrup, carefully remove the pan from the heat and dip the bottom in cold water to arrest the temperature rise. Carry out the test. If the right stage has not been reached, return the pan to the heat and continue boiling.

8 As soon as the required temperature has been reached, remove the pan from the heat and dip the bottom in cold water.

• TESTING THE TEMPERATURE OF A SYRUP •

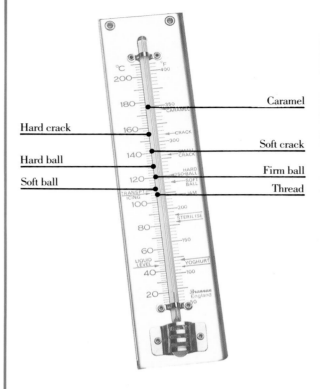

Hard crack

Hard ball

Soft ball

Caramel

Soft crack

Firm ball

Thread

See page 14 for information on different types of sugar

Soft ball 234-240°F

Dip the pan in cold water. Drop a small amount of the syrup into a bowl of very cold water, roll it into a ball in the water, then lift it out.

If the syrup forms a ball whilst in the water but becomes soft and flattens under slight pressure when removed from the water, the correct stage has been reached.

Used for fondants and fudge.

Hard ball 250-266°F

Dip the pan in cold water. Drop a small amount of the syrup into very cold water, form it into a ball in the water, then lift it out.

If the ball holds its shape under slight pressure but is still quite sticky, the correct temperature has been reached.

Used for nougat and marshmallows.

Soft crack 270-290°F

Dip the pan in cold water. Drop a small amount of the syrup into very cold water. Remove it between the fingers then gently separate them.

If the syrup forms threads that are hard but not brittle the correct stage has been reached.

Used for humbugs.

Thread 223-236°F

Dip the pan in cold water. Using a teaspoon, take a small amount of the syrup then gently and slowly pour it over the rim of the spoon.

If a thin thread forms the correct temperature has been reached.

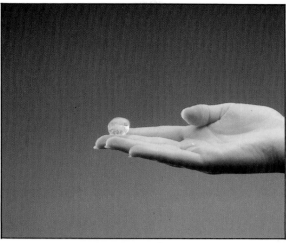

Firm ball 244-250°F

Dip the pan in cold water. Drop a small amount of the syrup into very cold water, roll it into a ball in the water, then lift it out.

If a ball holds its shape when lifted from the water but loses it as it warms up, the correct temperature has been reached.

Used for caramels.

Hard crack 300-310°F

Dip the pan in cold water. Drop a little of the syrup into very cold water, then remove it.

If it is hard and brittle the correct stage has been reached.

Used for hard toffee and rock.

Caramel 320-350°F

Dip the pan in cold water. Pour a small amount from a spoon onto a white plate. A golden honey indicates a light caramel, a golden amber color a dark caramel. If the syrup darkens beyond this stage it will begin to taste bitter.

Used for pralines.

F·U·D·G·E

The sugar syrup for fudge is boiled to the soft ball stage and is then beaten to encourage crystallization of the sugar and give the fudge its characteristic texture and appearance. These can, in fact, be changed slightly by beating the syrup at different times—immediately after it has been cooked or after it has been left to cool. Firmer candies with a more granular texture will result from beating in hot syrup whilst smooth fudge is the outcome of leaving the syrup to cool.

Stir fudge mixtures with a high milk or cream content to prevent them sticking and burning, and be sure to use a large enough saucepan as they will boil up considerably. (For a selection of fudge recipes, see pages 98-109.)

1 Place the thermometer in hot water to warm it. Oil the pan.

2 Gently heat the sugar with the milk, cream or diced butter and any other ingredients according to the recipe, in a thick saucepan that has a capacity at least four times the volume of the ingredients, stirring with a wooden spoon until the sugar has dissolved and any butter or chocolate melted.

3 Bring to a boil, cover and boil for about 3 minutes.

4 Uncover and boil until the required temperature has been reached, stirring as necessary if the mixture has a high milk or cream content.

5 Dip the pan in cold water.

6 Either beat the mixture immediately with a wooden spoon until it begins to thicken and becomes lighter in color and loses its gloss, then quickly pour into the pan and leave until beginning to set. Or, leave the mixture to cool to about 122°F and starting to become opaque, then beat until it becomes paler and thickens (below).

7 Pour into the pan and leave to set.

8 Mark into squares and leave to set completely.

9 Break into pieces and store in an airtight container between layers of waxed paper.

F·O·N·D·A·N·T

Fondant consists essentially of a mass of minute sugar crystals surrounded by a saturated sugar syrup. The creamy, smooth, melting texture is achieved through a series of precise stages, the first of which is the addition of glucose to the syrup to make sure that the sugar crystals formed during the later stages remain small so keeping the fondant smooth (glucose keeps the fondant softer for longer than would cream of tartar or another acid). The next stage is when the hot syrup is poured into a pool and the edges folded inwards to cool it quickly and evenly before it is 'worked' to develop the crystallization of the sugar. To free it of lumps the fondant is kneaded, like a dough for bread. It must then be left for at least 12 hours for the sugar crystals to undergo their final change, softening the fondant.

4 Using a dampened metal scraper or large metal spatula, lift the edges of the pool of syrup and fold them to the center. Repeat until the syrup becomes glossy and viscous and has a faint yellow color. (below)

1 Sprinkle an even coating of cold water over a marble slab or other suitable work surface.
2 Prepare a sugar, incorporating glucose, to 240°F, the soft ball stage.

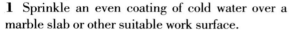

3 Dip the saucepan in cold water then quickly pour the syrup into a pool onto the surface and leave to cool for a few minutes.

5 Using a dampened wooden spatula work the mixture in a continuous figure of eight action for 5–10 minutes.

6 Stir until it becomes white and crumbly and the stirring is extremely difficult.

7 With lightly moistened hands, form a ball of fondant then knead it by pushing half of the ball away from you with the heel of one hand, fold the half back into the lump using a metal scraper or metal spatula and repeat in a flowing action for 5–10 minutes until the mixture is free of lumps and feels smooth.

8 Form the fondant into a ball, place it on a dampened plate, cover with a damp cloth to prevent the surface drying out and leave in a cool place for at least 12 hours.

• FONDANT-DIPPED FRUITS •

1 Fruits that have a stem or stalk – hold the fruit by the stem or stalk then dip it into the melted fondant so that it is about three-quarters coated.

4 Portions of fruit without stems – place the fruit on a dipping fork and lower it into the melted fondant. Turn it over so that it is completely coated.

2 Lift it out, allowing the excess to drain off and dip in sugar.

5 Lift the fruit out on the dipping fork, tap the fork lightly on the side of the bowl then draw the bottom of the fork across the edge of the bowl. Carefully transfer the fruit to waxed paper and leave to dry.

3 Leave the fruit on waxed paper to dry.

C·A·R·A·M·E·L·S

The traditional mellow, soft, creamy flavor of caramel candies is obtained by the addition of milk, or milk products such as cream, evaporated or condensed milk, and butter, and not, as the name suggests, by caramelizing the sugar. The characteristic chewy, moist texture comes from boiling the syrup as far as the firm ball stage, 244-250°F. However, the degree of firmness can be varied by taking the syrup to different points within the firm-hard ball range – the nearer to the top of the range, the firmer the candy.

It is especially important when making caramels to use a sufficiently large saucepan because the mixture expands considerably as it boils. Because of their milk, cream or butter content, caramels are liable to stick to the saucepan and therefore burn, so stirring becomes a necessity. Their thickening effect on the syrup provides some protection against crystallization of the sugar, but for a complete safeguard another anti-crystallizing agent (see page 18) is usually added as well. (A selection of caramel recipes may be found on pages 110-15.)

1 Line the base of a pan with a piece of oiled waxed paper.

2 Gently heat the sugar with the milk, cream or diced butter and anti-crystallizing agent in a heavy saucepan that has a capacity at least four times the volume of the ingredients.

3 Stir with a wooden spoon until the sugar has dissolved and any butter melted.

4 Bring to a boil, cover and boil for about 3 minutes.

5 Put the warmed thermometer in place and boil, stirring gently occasionally and taking care not to knock the thermometer, until the syrup reaches the required temperature.

6 Dip the saucepan in cold water to prevent the temperature rising further, then pour the caramel into the pan.

7 Leave to cool. Mark it into pieces when just beginning to set and before it becomes too hard. Oiling the knife will prevent sticking.

8 When the caramel is completely cold and firm, turn it out of the pan, remove the paper and divide it into the marked pieces. Wrap the caramel pieces in cellophane or waxed paper.

M·A·R·S·H·M·A·L·L·O·W·S

The basis for marshmallows is a syrup boiled to the hard ball stage, 250-266°F. Gelatin and stiffly beaten egg white are incorporated to transform it into softly set airy clouds.

The syrup with the dissolved gelatin must be poured into the egg whites in a slow, thin, steady stream, and the whites must be whisked constantly otherwise the weight of the syrup will knock the air bubbles out of them. A food mixer is therefore a great boon, but failing that, place the bowl containing the egg whites on a damp cloth to hold it steady. Whisking must continue until the mixture is very fluffy and light before it can be left to set. For this, an oiled pan well dusted with a mixture of sifted cornstarch and confectioners' sugar is used. All the surfaces of marshmallows are coated in cornstarch/confectioners' sugar to prevent them sticking together. (See page 82 for Marshmallows recipes.)

1 Prepare the pan.

2 Boil a syrup to the hard ball stage.

3 Meanwhile, mix the gelatin with a little cold water in a small bowl, place the bowl in a larger bowl of hot water and heat until dissolved.

4 Whisk the egg whites with a wire whisk (this gives a greater volume than a rotary or electric whisk) until stiff peaks are formed.

5 Add the gelatin to the syrup.

6 Then pour the syrup into the egg whites in a slow, thin, steady stream down the sides of the bowl.

7 Continue to whisk the mixture until it is very fluffy and light and just holds its shape firmly but is still thin enough to turn into the pan without difficulty. This may take 15-20 minutes.

8 Turn the mixture into the pan, lightly smoothing it out evenly and leveling the surface with a metal spatula. Leave to set.

9 Sift an even coating of cornstarch mixed with confectioners' sugar onto the work surface. Loosen around the sides of the pan containing the marshmallow with a small knife then invert the marshmallow onto the prepared surface.

10 Lightly coat the top and sides with cornstarch/ confectioners' sugar. Cut into pieces using a large, oiled knife or sharp scissors or oiled metal cutters.

11 Coat the sides of the pieces with cornstarch/ confectioners' sugar, then place on a wire rack to dry.

P·U·L·L·E·D C·A·N·D·I·E·S

The technique of 'pulling' is used to produce humbugs, rock and taffies. It involves forming syrup that has been boiled to 266-290°F, the hottest hard ball to soft crack stage, into a sausage shape, after it has been cooled slightly, then repeatedly pulling, folding and twisting it to incorporate a mass of tiny air bubbles, and give a shiny, silvery appearance. It requires strength and stamina – and hands that can withstand high temperatures as it is essential to work the syrup whilst it is as hot as possible because it looses pliability as it cools.

1 Prepare the syrup to the required temperature and oil a marble slab or other suitable surface.

2 Dip the saucepan in cold water then pour the syrup quickly into a pool on the surface. Leave it to cool briefly until a light skin forms on the surface.

3 Using an oiled metal scraper or large metal spatula, lift the edges of the pool of syrup and fold them into the center. Repeat until the syrup is just cool enough to handle.

4 With oiled hands, to prevent sticking, and the scraper or metal spatula, form the syrup into a sausage shape. Lift it up with your hands and pull it out to about 18 inches. Fold it back together and repeat the pulling and folding until the syrup changes from being soft and slightly sticky to a firmer, more shiny texture. Fold the pulled syrup in half, twist the two strands together then pull the twisted sausage out until it is about ½ inch in diameter. Repeat the folding, twisting and pulling until it becomes opaque, shiny and is no longer pliable. This may take up to 20 minutes.

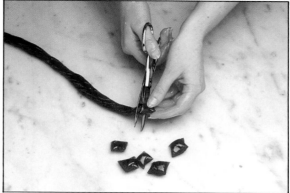

6 Using strong oiled scissors cut across the rope to form cushion shapes.

7 Wrap the candies in cellophane or waxed paper and store in an airtight container.

5 Fold the stretched-out sausage in half then in half again and gently twist the four strands together. Pull out again, gently twisting.

• DUAL-COLORED BOILED CANDIES •

The 'pulling' technique can also be used to make dual-colored boiled candies. They can either be made by combining 'ropes' of two different colored syrups, one pulled until it is opaque and pearlized, the other left shiny and translucent; or by dividing a syrup in half and pulling one half until it is pale but leaving the other half shiny then twisting the two together.

1 Oil a work surface.

2 Prepare a syrup using a brown sugar.

3 Pour the syrup into two pools onto the surface. As the edges of the pools begin to cool slightly, lift them and fold them into the center using an oiled metal scraper or large metal spatula.

4 With oiled hands, form one pool into a sausage shape, then pull, fold and twist it as in step 4 on page 30.

5 With oiled hands form the second pool into a sausage then pull it to form a similar length to the first, without working it so that its color hardly changes.

6 Lay the two pieces side by side, twist them together, then fold the length that is formed over and over to make a short rope.

7 Gently but firmly and quickly and giving a twist, pull along the length of the rope to produce a long, thin, twisted, even strand.

8 Using lightly oiled scissors cut into pieces giving the rope a half turn towards you so the pieces have triangular surfaces.

9 Store in an airtight container between layers of waxed paper.

N·O·U·G·A·T

There are two cooking processes involved in the preparation of nougat. The first is the boiling of the sugar syrup to the soft crack stage, 280°F; the second, a much more gentle one, 'sets' the stiffly beaten egg whites that have been added. As soon as the mixture thickens, it must be removed from the heat to avoid overcooking. To achieve the unique, compact chewy texture, one more, very simple step is necessary – the mixture must be weighted down overnight.

The nuts that are included in nearly every nougat recipe must be warmed slightly otherwise they will cause premature, localized setting. Honey, another traditional ingredient in many nougat recipes, is added to the syrup near the end of its preparation, as its characteristic flavor is changed by cooking. (For a selection of nougat recipes, see pages 130-3.)

1 Line a pan with rice paper.

2 Melt the honey in a bowl placed over a saucepan of hot water.

3 Prepare a sugar syrup containing glucose to the soft crack stage.

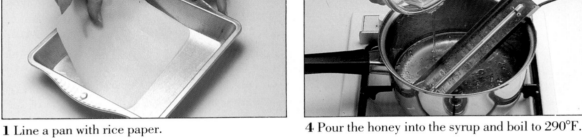

4 Pour the honey into the syrup and boil to 290°F.

5 Dip the saucepan in cold water.

6 Whisk the egg whites stiffly then pour the syrup into them in a slow, thin, steady stream, whisking constantly.

7 Place the bowl over a pan of just simmering water and whisk until the mixture becomes firm.

8 Remove from the heat, stir in the warmed nuts, cherries and candied angelica.

9 Pour into the pan, and spread out evenly.

10 Cover with rice paper, place a board on top and place weights on the board. Leave overnight to set.

11 Turn the nougat out of the pan, trim away excess rice paper and cut the nougat into squares or fingers using a large sharp knife. Wrap in cellophane and store in an airtight container.

C·H·O·C·O·L·A·T·E W·O·R·K

The chocolate for 'chocolates' should be the best that you can buy. It is just not worth spending the time to make candies from cheap brands of chocolate, cheap 'cooking' chocolate sold in unlabeled bags, or chocolate-flavored cake coverings. Special 'dipping' chocolate is available from good confectioners, or use a good quality dessert chocolate. For the most 'chocolatey' flavor use the least sweetened or bitter variety of semisweet chocolate. (A selection of chocolate recipes may be found on pages 70-3.)

• MELTING CHOCOLATE •

It is vital that the chocolate is melted with care, so don't rush it.

1 Chop the chocolate so that it will melt more quickly and evenly. Put it into a bowl placed over a saucepan of hot but not boiling water, making sure that the bottom of the bowl does not touch the water. (A heat-resistant glass bowl will enable you to check easily whether the water is bubbling and whether the bottom of the bowl is clear of the water.)

2 Remove the saucepan from the heat and stir the chocolate occasionally as it softens until it is free of lumps. Then stir it until it is smooth and liquid. Do not allow the temperature to rise higher than 120°F otherwise the flavor of the chocolate will be spoilt. spoilt.

3 Leave the chocolate to cool and therefore thicken slightly before using it. Once the right coating consistency is reached, keep the temperature constant by putting the bowl over hot water or removing it, as necessary. Throughout the process make sure that no steam or drop of water gets into the chocolate as it will spoil the candies.

It is especially important when working with chocolate to remember that it will not adhere to a wet or sticky surface, so make sure that any mold to be lined or any ingredient to be coated is completely dry – make caramels, fondants and marzipans a day in advance to give the outside a chance to dry out.

• DIPPING •

1 Melt the chocolate. Place one center at a time in the chocolate, turn it over gently with a fork then lift it out on the prongs.

2 Tap the fork on the rim of the bowl then draw the underside of the fork over the rim to remove any drips of chocolate.

3 Gently put the candy onto a tray lined with waxed paper and leave to dry.

4 Repeat with the remaining centers, keeping a check on the temperature of the chocolate to make sure that it does not become too hard.

• DECORATING CHOCOLATES •

This must be done whilst the chocolate is still wet.

• SIMPLE RIDGE •

Place the back of the prongs of a fork flat on the candy, chocolate, then lightly draw it over the surface to leave a ridge of chocolate.

• A SERIES OF PARALLEL LINES •

Place the back of the prongs of a fork flat on the sweet, then raise the fork straight upwards slightly, taking with it threads of chocolate to form ridges. Then carefully draw the fork straight backwards towards you.

• A CIRCLE ON A ROUND SHAPE •

Place a round dipping fork – or similar circular shape such as the end of a long kebab skewer – on the surface of the candy. Raise it straight upwards slightly, taking threads of chocolate with it to form a ridge, then carefully draw the fork or skewer straight backwards towards you.

• PIPING •

Fill a waxed paper pastry bag with melted chocolate of a contrasting color to the sweet, snip off the end of the bag then pipe fine lines over the surface of the candy.

• EASY LIQUEUR OR COCKTAIL CHOCOLATES •

1 Spoon a little melted chocolate into small foil candy cases, then gently tip and rotate the case to coat the sides evenly with chocolate. Pour any excess chocolate back into the bulk of the chocolate. Leave the cases to set.

2 Drop small blobs of chocolate on waxed paper equal to the number of cases. Spread the blobs out to small circles to fit the tops of the cases. Leave to set.

3 Fill the cases with the chosen spirit, liqueur or cocktail based on a spirit or liqueur.

4 Carefully lift the chocolate circles from the waxed paper.

5 To fix the lids, use a fine artist's or make-up brush, point of a sharp knife, or pastry bag. Run a little melted chocolate around the edge of the cases, then press the lids lightly in place and leave to set.

• MOLDED SHAPES •

1 Melt some chocolate – the amount will depend on the size of the mould, or moulds, bearing in mind that the larger the mould the thicker the chocolate case should be. (see step 4)

2 Make sure the mold is completely clean and dry, then spoon in some chocolate. Tip and rotate the mold so the chocolate flows to coat the sides completely and evenly.

3 Pour the excess chocolate back into the bulk of the chocolate, then leave the mold upside down on waxed paper to dry.

4 If the mold is large, apply a second, even a third layer, once the first one has set, to build up the right degree of thickness.

5 When the chocolate is hard, carefully remove any excess chocolate from the edges with a razor blade or sharp knife.

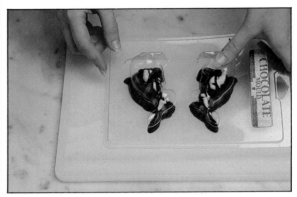

6 Gently tap the molds to release the cases of set chocolate.

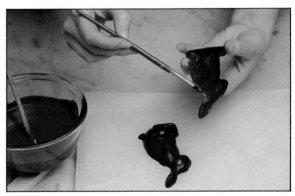

7 Spread a thin layer of melted chocolate over the rim of one of the cases, holding it steady on waxed paper. Place the second case on the first, again using waxed paper to shield the chocolate from the hands. Gently press the two halves together.

8 Decorate the outside with piped chocolate, crystallized flowers etc.

P·R·E·P·A·R·I·N·G   N·U·T·S

Nuts for candies must be perfectly dry, and when used for nougat or praline, they should be warmed slightly in a low oven so that they do not cause localized cooling and crystallization of the syrup. It is important also to prepare nuts properly before use. In particular, the fine skin that fits closely around each nut must be removed. (A selection of 'nutty candies' recipes may be found on pages 84-91.)

• ALMONDS •

1 Pour boiling water over the nuts, leave for a minute, then pour the water off.

• HAZELS AND BRAZILS •

1 Skins are easy to remove if the nuts are spread out on a baking tray and placed in an oven preheated to 325°F for 10 minutes.
2 Place the nuts in a colander and rub them with a cloth – the skins should flake off and fall through the holes.

2 It should then be easy to 'pop' the nuts out of the skins, whilst they are still warm.

3 If the skins remain firmly in place or if they cool, repeat the steeping process.

C·R·Y·S·T·A·L·L·I·Z·E·D
C·O·N·F·E·C·T·I·O·N·S

Crystallizing is the candy-lover's favorite method of preserving a variety of suitable fruits, flowers and fruit rinds, using a number of different techniques. Crystallized confections must be kept dry so pack them in an airtight container between layers of waxed paper and keep in a cool place. (For a selection of candied and crystallized fruit recipes, see pages 92-97.)

• FRUITS •

The crystallizing of fruits is a lengthy process that must be done gradually over a number of days – about 14 – yet it is very simple to do. The results of your own crystallizing can be delicious as well as immensely satisfying, especially if you use fruits or flowers from your garden.

Fruits for crystallizing should be ripe, but firm, in perfect condition and free of blemishes. Small fruits such as cherries, apricots and plums can be left whole but should be pricked all over with a needle to allow the syrup to penetrate. Larger fruits such as a pineapple or peaches, which are peeled and cut into pieces, do not need to be pricked. Soft fruits such as raspberries and strawberries are unsuitable as they disintegrate.

Candied fruits are crystallized fruits that have been dipped in a syrup to give them a glossy finish.

• FLOWERS •

The crystallizing process for flowers is much quicker than that for fruits but the initial preparation can be time-consuming as the entire surface of each petal must be painted evenly with gum arabic (available from drugstores.)

Small flowers such as violets and rose geraniums can be left whole, but larger ones, of which roses are the most popular example, are divided into petals. They must be in good condition, fresh and perfectly dry.

• FRUIT RINDS •

Rinds, from citrus fruits, are parboiled before being crystallized by simmering in a syrup to avoid a bitter taint to the finished candy.

• CRYSTALLIZING FRUITS •

1 Prepare the chosen fruit, then poach until just tender.

2 Transfer the fruit to a wire tray placed over a shallow tray and leave to drain.

3 Pour a syrup, made from 300ml/½ pint of the poaching liquor and 125g/6oz sugar, over the fruit that has been placed in a shallow tray.

4 Using a pancake turner, transfer the fruit to a wire rack, placed over a shallow tray.

5 Increase the concentration of the syrup by dissolving a further ¼ cup of sugar in it.

• CRYSTALLIZING FLOWERS •

1 Using a soft paint brush, coat flower petals with a mixture of gum arabic, rose water and food coloring.

2 Sift superfine sugar over the petals and leave on a wire rack in a warm place until dry and brittle.

M·A·R·Z·I·P·A·N

Homemade marzipan is an amenable chameleon amongst candies. It can be rolled, molded, cut and teased into a cornucopia of shapes from mushrooms to chequerboards. At the drop of a liquid food color it can be transformed into a rainbow of hues and tints. For uncooked and boiled methods see page 116.

· MARZIPAN CHEQUERBOARD ·

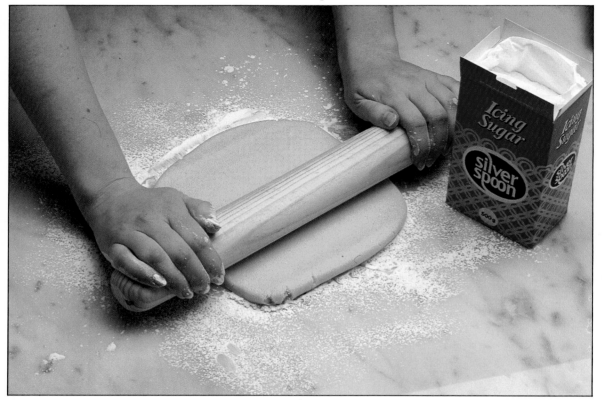

1 Roll out each piece of marzipan separately on a work surface lightly sprinkled with confectioners' sugar to a rectangle about ¼ inch thick.

2 Brush one piece with lightly beaten egg white.

3 Lay the second piece on top and pass a rolling pin lightly over the top to gently press the pieces together.

4 After trimming the edges of the rectangle with a sharp knife, cut it lengthways into 3 strips of equal width.

5 Brush the top of one strip lightly with lightly beaten egg white.

6 Place another strip on top, making sure that it is completely lined up. Repeat with the remaining strip.

7 Cut the stack lengthways into 4 strips with a long, sharp knife.

8 Lay one strip flat and place a second strip on the first, turning it over so the colors are reversed. Brush with egg white and repeat with the remaining strips, making sure the colors always alternate.

9 Cut into slices using a sharp knife then leave to dry on waxed paper for a few hours.

C·O·N·T·A·I·N·E·R·S A·N·D W·R·A·P·P·I·N·G·S

Homemade candies do not need to have any adornment – however, pretty or inventive packaging or wrapping can enhance the sense of occasion and 'specialness'.

• GLASS JARS•

Clear glass jars with ground glass or even screw-top closures are ideal for showing off candies that do not crush easily.

If giving the candies as a present tie a ribbon and bow around the neck of the jar and decorate the body of the jar with cut-out shapes of colored paper.

•INDIVIDUALLY• WRAPPED CANDIES

Candies can be wrapped individually in clear cellophane that will allow the color and sparkle of the candy to show through, or a colored cellophane, perhaps with an inner covering of foil, can be used. Plain thin aluminum foil, or colored or decorated foils make very bright and attractive wrappings.

▼

• GIFT BOXES AND• ENVELOPES

A wide variety of boxes and other containers can be bought from good stationers.

If the candies are likely to be crushed or squashed easily separate the layers of candies with a sheet of card or corrugated paper.

For that extra special touch compose a matching set.

•LACY CONES•

▲ *Cones to hold candies can also be made from decorative doilies. Very lacy white ones can look particularly effective if lined with plain material, but gold or silver ones can be left unlined. Simply form the doily into a cone shape and secure in place with staples. Thread a colored ribbon through the top row of holes.*

•CERAMIC DISHES•

There is an extensive range of attractive ceramic dishes available which are very popular as gifts. One that can be filled with home-made candies will give the present a personal touch. A genuine large shell could also be used.

•BASKETS AND OTHER• CONTAINERS

Wicker bread baskets or small sewing baskets can be padded and lined with pretty paper and material (this could be trimmed with ribbon or broderie anglaise), encased in clear cellophane and finished with a bow.

Other useful containers include shallow foil dishes, disposable plastic and polystyrene pots and trays used for dairy products and vegetables. Cover with paper or material, add some decorative adhesive shapes and finish with bows (the ready-tied adhesive ones are handy) and ribbons.
▼

•CONES•

Cut out equal sized squares of waxed and decorative paper. Place the colored paper with the pattern side down and cover with the waxed paper. Form into a cone by holding two opposite corners and rolling them together towards you. Secure the corners with colored staples or glue.

•TOYS•

A container that is fun to play with after the candies are eaten makes a good present for children.

C·H·R·I·S·T·M·A·S G·I·F·T·S

Christmas present giving can be notoriously difficult with many hours spent thinking and searching for just the right present. Yet with homemade candies it is so easy to hit upon an ideal gift every time, whether it is just a small token or, something very special.

•CARTONS AND BOXES•

◄ *At Christmas time it is possible to buy all manner of pretty, decorated gift cartons and boxes and what better gift to fill them with than homemade candies.*
Homemade Christmas *boxes can be made from any box over-wrapped with Christmas paper or, from a strip and disc of card stuck together and covered with Christmas paper.*

•WINE GLASSES•
A more sophisticated Christmas stocking – from an everyday wine glass right through to expensive crystal. Cocktail or liqueur chocolates and truffles seem the obvious choice for filling the glass. Decorate with a bow and a sprig of holly. ▶

•CHRISTMAS STOCKING•
A selection of wrapped candies makes an ideal stocking filler for children of all ages.
▼

•TABLE OR TRAY• DECORATIONS
Make attractive table or tray decorations with edible centers of soft pale green fondant rolled in chopped nuts. The leaves and flowers are made from colored candy cases. ▲

•DECORATED CANDIES•
Boxes of homemade candies can be decorated with colored marzipan or fondant.
▼

• MUGS AND DISHES•

A filling of homemade candies add a personal touch to bought mugs and ceramic dishes. ▶

•SHAPED CANDIES•

Marzipan and fondant can be colored and flavored, if liked, then formed into Christmasy shapes such as Christmas trees and stars to decorate cake or pudding plates. ▼

• CHRISTMAS CRACKERS•

Crackers are easy to make at home. Cut out equal sized rectangles of waxed and colored cellophane, crepe, or decorative paper. Place the colored paper, pattern side down, with the waxed on top. Cut out a piece of card, the same width as the paper but only 1/3 of the length. Place across the waxed paper. Form into a roll with the card inside. Twist one end about 2 inches from the end and fill the tube with candies. Twist the other end. Decorate with ribbons, bows and decorative cut-out shapes. ▶

•CANDY BAGS•

Cut circles about 6 inches in diameter, depending on the number of candies and their size, from crepe, tissue, cellophane paper or pretty fabric. If the candies are not wrapped cut a lining of waxed paper for material bags. Trim the edge of the fabric with lace for an attractive finish. Place the candies in the center of the circle and gather up the paper or material over them. Tie with a ribbon and finish with a bow. ◀

•HANGING CANDIES•

Individually wrapped candies can be tied with bows and ribbons to make decorations for the tree or elsewhere around the house. ▶

V·A·L·E·N·T·I·N·E GIFTS

As it is well-known that in giving food we are fulfilling a basic desire to please those we love and care about, then to offer a gift that is indulgent, irresistible and personally made must be the most sincere and meaningful token of affection.

•CAR•

Presents that show a degree of fondness or caring, yet are not too overt, can be the most difficult to choose. A perfect solution is a gift that matches the person's hobby or interest, such as a car plus some homemade candies all tied up with a simple bow of ribbon decorated with hearts.

▼

•BOXES•

Ordinary square and rectangular boxes with heart shapes on them can be bought but it is also easy to create the same effect yourself. Either cover a plain box with paper that has a heart design printed on it or, stick cut-out heart shapes on a plain box. A tin can also be covered or decorated in the same way. ▶

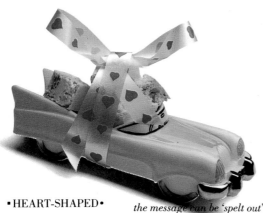

•HEART-SHAPED• BOXES

Heart-shaped boxes are available from most stationers. Fill with homemade candies and add a red rose. ▶

•HEART-SHAPED• CANDIES

Actions speak louder than words and a box of heart-shaped homemade candies says so much so simply. Or,

the message can be 'spelt out' by decorating the candies in appropriate letters formed from marzipan or fondant or piped chocolate. ▼

LARGE HEART-
• SHAPED CONTAINER •

A large heart-shaped container can be made from a heart-shaped cake pan, placed on a base of stiff cardboard, cut to shape and then covered with red satin, crepe paper or foil. The bottom of the container can be padded with tissue paper. Liqueur or spirit-flavored fondant chocolates finished with crystallized flowers, or luscious truffles are the most suitable candies for such a lavish present. Add a bow of red ribbon and wrap the container and candies in clear cellophane.

Small heart-shaped containers can be made in the same way using heart-shaped cookie cutters. The candies can be 'tied in' with ribbon crossed over them and tied into a big bow.

• SUSPENDED CANDY •
BAGS

For a glamorous 'fun' gift form small candy bags from gold net, perhaps one that has a heart-shaped decoration on it. Decorate the filled bag with a small heart-shaped brooch and tie it up with ribbon decorated with hearts.

• CERAMIC DISHES •

Search for heart-shaped ornamental dishes for pastel-colored fondant candies. Or, for a gift that is also functional – ideal for the enthusiastic·cook – use heart-shaped white cœur à la crème molds, available from kitchen-ware stores and departments of large stores.

E·A·S·T·E·R G·I·F·T·S

Easter is a bright, cheery time, a time for giving and for enjoying yourself. And what better way to capture the air of enthusiasm and generosity than with batches of homemade candies.

• MUGS•
◄ *Combine a useful present with one that is delicious to eat. Pack fine strips of colored cellophane paper in the bottom of the mug to form a 'nest' and over-wrap candies that are piled up with cellophane paper to hold them in place.*

• DAFFODIL CANDIES•
Give an Easter air to chocolates, fondants or marzipans by decorating them with small crystallized primroses or small seasonal flowers, such as daffodils or narcissi formed out of colored marzipan or fondant. ►

•CERAMIC DISHES•
Easter is associated with bright yellows, fresh greens, lambs and daffodils, so for an Easter present select a dish suitably colored and decorated. ►

• EGG CUPS•
In the months approaching Easter, egg cups and similar small ceramic dishes shaped with chicks or small rabbits become available in the stores. These are ideal for filling with chocolate eggs or other homemade candies.
▼

•DECORATING EASTER• EGGS

Easter eggs can be made to look as good as they taste in many ways. They can be wrapped in decorated foil; crystallized flowers or flowers formed out of fondant or marzipan can be 'stuck' onto the surface using a little melted chocolate; a design can be piped onto the surface or around the seam; or the egg can simply be tied in a pretty bow.

• CHRISTENING •

Easter is a popular time for christenings. For a gratifying yet lasting present give a porcelain ornament plus some homemade candies. ▶

• EASTER SHAPES •

Chicks can be made from marzipan, colored yellow, with the beaks molded out of orange marzipan. Colored feathers can be inserted to act as tails, with legs and feet made from coated wire.

Small rabbits can also be formed from colored marzipan. Their tails can be made from cotton wool or make-up removing balls.

Easter eggs can, of course, be made from molded chocolate. They can also be formed from colored marzipan or fondant, or even from chocolate truffle mixtures. Give a box filled with a selection of eggs.

• EGG TRAY •

A cardboard egg tray provides an obvious seasonal container for small Easter eggs nestling on a bed of 'straw' made out of fine strands of tissue paper. Do not forget to over-wrap the tray and eggs with cellophane paper. Smaller gifts can be made in the same way using the bottom portion of small size egg boxes. ▼

• CHOCOLATE RABBIT •

◀ Molds are available for making chocolate rabbits in the same way as Easter eggs. Buy a small mold as well as a large one to make a family of rabbits.

Finish the rabbit with a ribbon tied in a bow around the neck.

B·I·R·T·H·D·A·Y G·I·F·T·S

With the help of a supply of homemade candies there is no need to ever despair of what to give someone for a present. Nearly everyone has a hobby or interest that can provide the spark of inspiration to turn a 'useful' everyday item into something rather special – homemade candies show that care and thought have gone into the present.

•SUGAR MICE•

Instructions for making sugar mice are given on page 157, but as many people are animal lovers adapt the instructions to make an appropriate type of animal such as a pet dog or cat. Tie a ribbon and bow around its neck.
▼

•TANKARD•

Beer drinkers are not the only people who would appreciate a glass mug or tankard – 1¼ cup sizes are useful for fruit juices or other soft drinks, such as Bucks Fizz (sparkling wine and orange juice), Black Velvet (Guinness and sparkling wine) or Pimms.
▼

•LOLLIPOPS•

Choose three or four flavorings and appropriate colorings of lollipops as an alternative to candies. Kids will love to find their favorite lollies in a bright new pair of wellies.
▶

•TRAIN•

When buying toys for children, choose ones that can be filled with candies.

Add a shipment of edible freight to the ever-popular toy train set. ▲

•NUMBERS•

Make numbers from colored and flavored marzipan to correlate to the relevant birthday, or as an imaginative gift for a child who is learning to count. ▲

• CERAMIC DISH •
With a little searching glass
or ceramic dishes can be
found to match up to all
manner of hobbies and
interests – a fish would be

▲
suitable for an aquarium
enthusiast.

• GARDEN GNOME •
Ideal for the gardener. Fill
the barrow with candies
the gardener can suck or
chew whilst pondering over
his garden or, recovering
from strenuous digging. ▶

• INITIALS •
▲ Decorate candies with letters
formed from fondant or
marzipan or piped chocolate
and arrange them in a box so
they spell out the recipient's
name or a message.

• ARTISTS PALETTE •
◀ Colored candies provide
instant, edible splashes of
color and – hopefully –
inspiration for a work of art.

FOR THE SWEET-
• TOOTHED COOK •
Combine practicality with
indulgence for the sweet-
toothed cook – give
equipment that is needed for
making candies, a selection
of candies to illustrate just
how delicious homemade
ones can be, plus a copy of
this book.

• WATCH •
▲
Candies are a timeless gift,
when teamed with a watch
that will act as a lasting
memory of the care and
trouble that lay behind the
giving of the gift.

T·H·E
R·E·C·I·P·E·S

S·I·M·P·L·E C·A·N·D·I·E·S

There are many delicious candies that do not fall into the traditional categories, do not need any cooking, and can be made in a matter of moments. These are ideal for inexperienced cooks of all ages, and will easily get them into the swing of candy making. Alternatively, if you are short on time or need to provide candies in a hurry, any one of these simple candies will serve you well.

C·O·C·O·N·U·T I·C·E
(uncooked)

MAKES ABOUT 1½ lb
2/3 cup condensed milk
2 cups confectioners' sugar, sieved
2 cups shredded coconut
A few drops of pink food coloring

1 Dust a jelly roll pan or a square pan with extra confectioners' sugar.
2 Mix the condensed milk, confectioners' sugar and coconut together in a large bowl to give a fairly stiff mixture.
3 Divide in half, and add a few drops of food coloring to one half to give a delicate pink.
4 If using a rectangular pan, spread one mixture in one half, the other mixture in the other half, and press down firmly. If using a square pan, about 7 inch, press one mixture over the base and press down firmly, then spread the other mixture over the top and press down firmly.
5 Leave to set, then cut into fingers or cubes with a lightly oiled knife.
6 Wrap in waxed paper and store in an airtight container in a cool place.

C·H·E·S·T·N·U·T C·R·A·C·K·L·E·S

MAKES ABOUT 30
10 oz can unsweetened chestnuts, drained
2/3 cup milk
1 cup cake crumbs, rubbed through a sieve
¼ cup superfine sugar
1 tablespoon brandy
1 tablespoon heavy cream
1 cup sugar

1 Gently cook the chestnuts in the milk for 10 minutes.
2 Sieve into a bowl and beat in the sieved cake crumbs, the ¼ cup superfine sugar, brandy and cream.
3 With wetted fingers form into small balls.
4 Leave on silicone paper to allow a skin to form.
5 Gently heat the 1 cup sugar in a heavy saucepan, shaking it occasionally, until the sugar has dissolved.
6 Increase the heat to 320-350°F and cook until it becomes a medium caramel color.
7 Remove from the heat and tilt the pan to form a pool of caramel, then lower in one chestnut ball at a time on a lightly oiled chocolate dipping fork, carving fork, or ordinary fork.
8 Place in small paper candy cases. Serve within a few hours.

• ABOVE •
Coconut Ice (top)
Chestnut Crackles (bottom)

• ABOVE •
Chocolate Nut Fudge
• OPPOSITE •
Praline Chocolate Layers

P·R·A·L·I·N·E C·H·O·C·O·L·A·T·E L·A·Y·E·R·S

MAKES ABOUT 50–60
1½ cups hazelnuts, lightly toasted
½ cup superfine sugar
1 tablespoon oil
1 lb semisweet chocolate
1⅓ cups white chocolate pieces
1½ tablespoons Kirsch
1 tablespoon Grand Marnier

1 Mix the nuts, sugar and oil together in a food processor or blender using on/off bursts until the mixture becomes an oily paste redolent of peanut butter. Scrape the bowl or goblet frequently.

2 Chop half the semisweet chocolate and melt it and the white chocolate separately in bowls placed over saucepans of hot water until their temperatures reach 110°F.

3 Beat half of the nut paste into each bowl of chocolate.

4 Add the Kirsch to the semisweet chocolate, the Grand Marnier to the white chocolate.

5 Divide each mixture in half and roll each piece out separately between 2 sheets of plastic wrap to a large rectangle. Turn the sheets over halfway through so that both sides will be flat.

6 Chill for about 10 minutes to firm up.

7 Remove the plastic wrap and stack the layers alternately on top of each other. Trim the edges using a large sharp knife.

8 Cut into strips about 1½ inches wide.

9 Grate the remaining semisweet chocolate and melt it in a bowl placed over a saucepan of hot water.

10 Spread the strips with melted chocolate, working in one direction only.

11 Leave on waxed paper to set then cut into pieces with an oiled knife. Store in an air-tight container in a cool place.

C·H·O·C·O·L·A·T·E N·U·T F·U·D·G·E
(uncooked)

MAKES ABOUT 1¾ lb
⅓ cup semisweet chocolate pieces
¾ cup soft cheese
1 tablespoon light cream
1½ lb confectioners' sugar, sieved
1 cup chopped nuts
A few drops of vanilla extract

1 Oil a pan approximately 7 inches square.

2 Melt the chocolate in a bowl placed over a saucepan of hot water.

3 Beat the cheese with the cream until smooth.

4 Work the confectioners' sugar into the cream and cheese mixture, then beat in the chocolate.

5 Stir in the nuts and vanilla extract, then pour into the pan.

6 Press down firmly, cover and chill until almost set.

7 Mark into squares with a sharp knife and chill for several hours.

8 Keep in an airtight container in the refrigerator for up to 3 days.

C·O·F·F·E·E A·N·D W·A·L·N·U·T C·R·E·A·M·S

MAKES ABOUT ¾ lb
Scant ¼ cup full fat soft cheese
Approximately 2 teaspoons good quality coffee extract
Approximately scant 2 cup confectioners' sugar, sifted
⅓ cup semisweet chocolate pieces
Walnut halves

1 Beat the cheese until smooth then beat in the coffee extract. Gradually beat in sufficient confectioners' sugar to give a stiff consistency.
2 Form the mixture into a smooth ball, then roll out on a surface lightly dusted with extra confectioners' sugar, using a rolling pin similarly dusted with confectioners' sugar, to ¼–½ inch thick.
3 Cut into 1 inch rounds with a cutter dusted with confectioners' sugar. Leave to dry.
4 Melt the chocolate in a small bowl placed over a saucepan of hot water.
5 Place a small teaspoon of chocolate on the top of each coffee cream. Press a walnut half on the chocolate while it is still soft, then leave to set.

C·H·O·C·O·L·A·T·E P·E·P·P·E·R·M·I·N·T C·R·E·A·M·S
(uncooked)

MAKES ABOUT ½ lb
1 egg white
Peppermint oil
Scant 2 cups confectioners' sugar
⅔ cup semisweet chocolate pieces

1 Lightly dust a work surface, rolling pin and a ½ inch cutter with extra confectioners' sugar.
2 Whisk the egg white until it is foamy.
3 Add about 4 drops of peppermint oil.
4 Mix in sufficient confectioners' sugar to give a stiff

but pliable paste.
5 Turn onto the work surface and knead until it is smooth and free of cracks.
6 Roll out to about ¼ inch thick.
7 Cut into circles with a cutter.
8 Melt the chocolate in a bowl placed over a saucepan of hot water.
9 Using a skewer to spear the candies, dip them into the chocolate to coat them, allowing excess chocolate to drain back into the bowl. Keep the chocolate at the right temperature and consistency by removing or returning it from or to the heat as necessary.
10 Leave the candies on a wire rack to set.

P·E·A·N·U·T B·U·T·T·E·R C·R·E·A·M·S

MAKES ABOUT 1 lb
¼ cup full fat soft cheese
Approximately 2 cups confectioners' sugar, sieved
3 tablespoons smooth peanut butter
1 tablespoon unsalted butter
A few drops of vanilla extract
Approximately ¼ cup unsalted peanuts, finely chopped

1 Beat the cheese until softened and smooth.
2 Gradually beat in the sugar, peanut butter, butter and vanilla extract to give a stiff consistency. If necessary add a little more confectioners' sugar.
3 Cover and chill the mixture for 1–2 hours.
4 Form into small balls and roll each ball in finely chopped peanuts.
5 Place in paper candy cases, cover and keep refrigerated for up to 4 days. Return to room temperature about 2 hours before eating.

• ABOVE •
Peanut Butter Creams (top)
Chocolate Peppermint Creams (center)
Coffee Walnut Creams (bottom)

T·R·U·F·F·L·E·S

Truffles combine simplicity with melting deliciousness. They are among the easiest and quickest of candies to make, yet can be the most mouthwatering, bringing true sophistication within the reach of even the most amateur of cooks.

There is a vast array of recipes for truffles. Chocolate is the common ingredient, but after that the choice is enormous: cream and liqueurs for dinner-party 'specials', butter, nuts or fruits or ground almonds in the form of marzipan as a base. They can also be made more economically with fine cake crumbs.

Truffles usually benefit from being kept for a few hours before being eaten, but they should not be kept for more than about 3 days, which provides a wonderful excuse for you to be greedy and unrestrained!

C·A·R·O·B T·R·U·F·F·L·E·S

MAKES ABOUT 10
3 tablespoons unsweetened carob powder
1 tablespoon instant coffee powder
2 tablespoons clear honey
1 tablespoon unsalted butter, diced
¼ cup skim milk powder
Carob powder flavored with ground cinnamon, for coating

1 Mix the carob and coffee powders together in a bowl.

2 Add the honey, place over a saucepan of hot water and heat until evenly blended.
3 Remove from the heat and mix in the butter and milk powder.
4 Cool a little, then form into small balls. Roll lightly in carob powder flavored with ground cinnamon.
5 Place in small paper candy cases. Cover and leave in a cool place overnight before eating.

C·O·C·O·N·U·T T·R·U·F·F·L·E·S

MAKES ABOUT 12
⅓ cup semisweet chocolate pieces
2 tablespoons light cream
Scant 1 cup confectioners' sugar, sifted
⅔ cup shredded coconut
Grated semisweet or white chocolate, for coating

1 Heat the ⅓ cup chocolate in a bowl placed over a saucepan of hot water until just melted.
2 Remove from the heat and beat in the cream.
3 Gradually work in the confectioners' sugar then the coconut.
4 Cover and chill until firm enough to handle.
5 Form into balls, coat in grated chocolate, and place in small paper candy cases.

• ABOVE •
*Coconut Truffles made with white and
semisweet chocolate.*
• OPPOSITE •
Carob Truffles

C·H·O·C·O·L·A·T·E M·A·R·Z·I·P·A·N T·R·U·F·F·L·E·S

MAKES ABOUT 1 lb
½ cup semisweet chocolate pieces
½ lb marzipan
5 tablespoons ground hazelnuts
A few drops of vanilla extract
2 teaspoons sweet Madeira, Marsala or sweet sherry
Unsweetened cocoa powder, for coating

1 Melt the chocolate in a bowl placed over a saucepan of hot water.
2 Mix the chocolate into the marzipan until it is just blended, then add the ground nuts, a few drops of vanilla extract, and the Madeira, Marsala or sherry.

3 Chill the mixture until it is firm enough to handle, then form into small balls and coat in cocoa powder.
4 Place in a small paper candy cases, cover and keep in a cool place for several hours before eating.

C·H·O·C·O·L·A·T·E H·A·Z·E·L·N·U·T T·R·U·F·F·L·E·S
(with butter)

MAKES ABOUT 40
1⅓ cups semisweet chocolate pieces
¾ cup unsalted butter, chopped
4 tablespoons heavy cream
Scant 1 cup confectioners' sugar, sieved
½ cup hazelnuts, very finely chopped
For the coatings
chocolate sprinkles
Unsweetened cocoa powder flavored with good quality instant coffee

1 Melt the chocolate and butter together in a bowl placed over a saucepan of hot water, stirring with a wooden spoon.
2 Remove from the heat, stir in the cream then gradually stir in the sugar and nuts.
3 Cover and leave in a cool place – not in the refrigerator – for at least 12 hours.
4 Form the mixture into small balls. Roll them in your hands so the warmth of the hands slightly melts the chocolate on the outside, which will help the coating to stick.
5 Roll each ball in one of the coatings and place in paper candy cases. Chill in the refrigerator until firm.

• ABOVE •
Chocolate Marzipan Truffles
• OPPOSITE •
Chocolate Hazelnut Truffles

• ABOVE •
Hazelnut Truffles
• OPPOSITE •
Cream Truffles

H·A·Z·E·L·N·U·T T·R·U·F·F·L·E·S
(with sponge cakes)

MAKES ABOUT 25
⅔ cup semisweet chocolate pieces
¼ cup unsalted butter, chopped
2 cups cake crumbs, rubbed through a sieve
Scant ½ cup confectioners' sugar, sifted
2 tablespoons cognac
½ cup hazelnuts, skinned and finely chopped
Approximately ½ cup chocolate sprinkles

1 Melt the chocolate in a bowl placed over a saucepan of hot water.
2 Stir in the butter.
3 Remove the bowl from the heat and beat in the cake crumbs, sugar and cognac.
4 Stir in the nuts then refrigerate until firm enough to mold.
5 With fingers lightly dusted with confectioners' sugar, form the mixture into small balls.

6 Roll the balls in chocolate sprinkles until evenly coated.
7 Place in paper candy cases and keep in a cool place for up to 4 days.

C·R·E·A·M T·R·U·F·F·L·E·S

MAKES ABOUT 30
1⅓ cups semisweet chocolate pieces
⅔ cup heavy cream
3 tablespoons cognac
Scant ¾ cup confectioners' sugar, sieved
1 teaspoon good quality instant coffee, dissolved in
1 tablespoon hot water and cooled
Unsweetened cocoa powder, for coating

1 Soften the chocolate in a bowl placed over a saucepan of hot water.
2 Rinse a heavy saucepan with cold water, pour in the cream and bring to a boil.
3 Strain the cream into the chocolate and stir until the chocolate has completely melted and the mixture is smooth.
4 Remove from the heat and leave to cool to room temperature.
5 Stir in the cognac, confectioners' sugar and cooled dissolved coffee.
6 Beat until smooth.
7 Cover and chill until the mixture is firm enough to mold.
8 Form into walnut-sized balls using two cold forks.
9 Roll the truffles lightly in cocoa powder to give them a thin coating.
10 Place in paper candy cases and chill in the refrigerator until firm.

• ABOVE •
Orange Truffles
• OPPOSITE •
Praline Rum Truffles

P·R·A·L·I·N·E R·U·M T·R·U·F·F·L·E·S

MAKES ABOUT 24

¼ cup superfine sugar
¼ cup finely chopped almonds
1 cup semisweet chocolate pieces
3 tablespoons dark rum
¼ cup unsalted butter, diced
3 tablespoons heavy cream
Unsweetened cocoa powder, for coating

1 Lightly oil a baking sheet.
2 Gently heat the sugar in a small heavy saucepan until it has melted and become golden in color.
3 Stir in the nuts.
4 Pour onto the baking sheet and leave for about 30 minutes to cool.
5 Crush the praline into coarse crumbs.
6 Heat the chocolate with the rum in a bowl placed over a saucepan of hot water, stirring occasionally, until it has just melted.
7 Remove the bowl from the heat and gradually beat in the butter then the cream.
8 Stir in the praline crumbs.
9 Leave in a cool place to firm up and become more manageable, then form into balls.
10 Roll them in cocoa powder or crushed praline to coat evenly, then place in small paper candy cases.
11 Keep in a cool place.

O·R·A·N·G·E T·R·U·F·F·L·E·S

MAKES ABOUT 35

1⅔ cups semisweet chocolate pieces
⅔ cup heavy cream
Scant ⅓ cup Grand Marnier
Finely grated rind of 1 orange
1 cup almonds, finely chopped
Sifted unsweetened cocoa powder, for coating

1 Soften the chocolate in a bowl placed over a saucepan of hot water.
2 Rinse a heavy saucepan with cold water, pour in the cream and bring to a boil.
3 Strain the cream into the chocolate and stir until the chocolate has completely melted and the mixture is smooth.
4 Remove from the heat and leave to cool to room temperature.
5 Beat in the Grand Marnier, orange rind and almonds.
6 Cover and chill until the mixture is firm enough to mold.
7 Form into walnut-sized balls using two cold forks.
8 Roll the truffles lightly in cocoa powder to give them a thin coating and decorate with candied orange slices.
9 Place in paper candy cases and chill in the refrigerator until firm.

C·H·O·C·O·L·A·T·E W·O·R·K

For most candy lovers, chocolates are the ultimate in confections. Fondants are fine, as are crystallized fruits, marzipans and caramels, but give them a dark, glossy coating and they become sublime, an indulgence impossible to ignore. (For illustrations of methods, see page 34.)

C·H·O·C·O·L·A·T·E C·O·A·T·E·D F·R·U·I·T·S A·N·D N·U·T·S

1 Drop the items to be coated individually into the melted chocolate, turn them over with a dipping fork, or ordinary fork, then lift out.

2 Tap the fork on the side of the bowl, then draw the underside of the fork across the rim of the bowl.
3 Carefully transfer the coated item to waxed paper and leave to dry.
4 Place in small paper candy cases, place in a single layer in a candy box and keep in a cool place.

• CHOCOLATE COATED MARZIPAN AND FONDANT •

1 Form the marzipan or fondant into the shapes required then leave to dry for 24 hours.
2 Drop the items to be coated individually into the melted chocolate, turn them over with a dipping fork, or ordinary fork, then lift out.
3 Tap the fork on the side of the bowl, then draw the underside of the fork across the rim of the bowl.
4 Carefully transfer the coated item to waxed paper and leave to dry.
5 Place in small paper candy cases, place in a single layer in a candy box and keep in a cool place.

• ABOVE •
Chocolate Coated Marzipan and Fondants
• OPPOSITE •
Chocolate Coated Fruit and Nuts

S·O·F·T C·E·N·T·E·R·E·D C·H·O·C·O·L·A·T·E

MAKES 24 CHOCOLATES
1⅓ cups semisweet or dipping chocolate pieces
6 oz fondant (page 146)
crystallized fruit, nut or peel, or brandied fruit
(pages 93 and 95)

1 Melt the chocolate (page 34).
2 Spoon a little of the chocolate into a small foil candy case, then gently tip and rotate the case to coat the base and sides evenly with chocolate.
3 Pour excess chocolate back into the bulk of the chocolate then leave the case to set.
4 Repeat with more cases.
5 Spoon a little melted fondant into each case, add a small piece of crystallized fruit, nut or peel or brandied fruit.
6 Cover with another layer of fondant and leave to set.
7 Spoon and spread a little more chocolate on top of the fondant to make a complete covering.
8 Leave to set, and store in a cool place.

• STRAWBERRY OR RASPBERRY CREAMS •
Make a small hole in the fondant, add a very small amount of strawberry or raspberry conserve, then seal the hole with fondant before covering.

• CHERRY CREAMS •
Flavor fondant with Kirsch and place a piece of candied cherry on the fondant before covering.

• COFFEE CREAMS •
Use coffee or coffee liqueur flavored fondant and decorate with walnut pieces while chocolate is wet.

• CHOCOLATE CREAMS •
Use chocolate flavored fondant and sprinkle chocolate sprinkles in the chocolate covering while it is wet, pipe chocolate scroll, using star tube, on top.

• CHOCOLATE HAZELNUT CREAMS •
Use chocolate flavored fondant and either sprinkle chopped hazelnuts on the covering while it is wet, or place whole or half a nut in the chocolate.

E·A·S·Y L·I·Q·U·E·U·R O·R C·O·C·K·T·A·I·L C·H·O·C·O·L·A·T·E·S

MAKES ABOUT 12 CHOCOLATES
⅔ cup semisweet or dipping chocolate pieces
¾ cup liqueur or cocktail (see method)
(For step-by-step illustrations, see page 37)

1 Melt the chocolate (page 34).
2 Spoon a little of the chocolate into a small foil candy case, then gently tip and rotate the case to coat the sides and base evenly with chocolate.
3 Pour excess chocolate back into the bulk of the chocolate, then leave the case to set.
4 Repeat with more cases.
5 Drop blobs of chocolate on waxed paper equal to the number of cases and spread the blobs out to circles to fit the tops of the cases. Leave to set.
6 Fill the cases with cognac, armagnac, port, sherry, whisky, rum, liqueur or a cocktail made from a spirit and a liqueur.
7 Carefully lift the chocolate circles from the paper.
8 Pipe or paint a little melted chocolate around the edge of each circle and carefully place in the cases. Press lightly in place and leave to set.

• ABOVE •
Easy Liqueur Chocolates
• OPPOSITE •
Soft centered Chocolates

F·O·N·D·A·N·T CREAM EGGS

Use approximately ½ lb milk or semisweet
chocolate per 2-3 4 inch high eggs
Approximately 1 lb plain boiled fondant
(see page 149)

1 Make up hollow medium size Easter egg, following the molding instructions on page 38, but do not remove the cases from the mold after the chocolate has set.
2 Soften a little boiled fondant (which should not be allowed to get too hot) and pour it into chilled chocolate mold, filling both sides.
3 Refrigerate until firm.
4 Turn the chocolate cases out of the molds carefully and seal them together with a little melted chocolate.

E·A·S·T·E·R EGGS

Use approximately 1 lb semisweet chocolate per
8 inch high eggs
½ lb per 2-3 4 inch high eggs
7 oz for one 7 inch high egg

1 Ensure that the mold is completely clean, free of grease and dry.
2 Melt the chocolate (see page 34).
3 Spoon some of the chocolate into the mold. Tip and rotate the mold so that the chocolate coats the sides completely.
4 Pour off any excess chocolate and leave the mold upside down on waxed paper to dry. If the molds are large, apply a second or even a third layer once the first has set, to build up the right degree of thickness.
5 When the chocolate is hard, carefully remove any excess from the edges with a razor blade or sharp knife, then run the point of the knife or blade between the rim of the chocolate and the mold.
6 Carefully ease the chocolate out of the mold.
7 Spread a thin layer of melted chocolate over the rim of one of the chocolate cases, holding the case steady on waxed paper. Place a second case on the first, again using waxed paper to shield the chocolate from the hands. Gently press the two halves together.
8 Decorate the shell with, for example, piped chocolate or crystallized flowers.

• ABOVE •
Easter Egg
• OPPOSITE •
Fondant Cream Eggs

J·E·L·L·I·E·S

The diversity of jellied candies ranges from the sparkling simplicity of fruit jellies to the sophistication of crème de menthe, from the Eastern promise of Turkish delight, to cloud-like marshmallows. Jellied candies can be cut into simple shapes after setting using a knife that has been wetted to prevent it sticking, or into more fancy shapes with wetted small cutters, or the liquid jelly can be poured on to a wetted fondant mat before being left to set to make jellies with a professional look.

F·R·U·I·T J·E·L·L·I·E·S

MAKES 1 lb
1 oz unflavored gelatin (4 envelopes)
⅔ cup clear fruit juice (eg, lemon, orange,
blackcurrant, strawberry, raspberry), strained if
necessary
6 tablespoons sugar
4 tablespoons liquid glucose
Food coloring (optional)
Superfine sugar (optional)

1 Wet a pan approximately 6 inches square.
2 Soften the gelatin in 4 tablespoons water.
3 Gently heat the fruit juice, sugar and glucose in a heavy saucepan until the sugar has dissolved, stirring with a wooden spoon.
4 Stir in the gelatin and continue to heat gently, stirring, until the gelatin has dissolved.
5 If the liquid is too pale add a few drops of appropriate food coloring.
6 Pour into the pan and leave to set in a cool place for at least 6 hours.
7 Turn the jelly out of the pan onto a cold work surface and cut into squares or shapes with a sharp knife or cutter.
8 Serve plain or roll in superfine sugar.
9 Sugar-coated jellies can be kept in a cool place in an airtight container for a few days.

O·R·A·N·G·E S·L·I·C·E·S

MAKES ABOUT ½ lb
¾ cup sugar
6 tablespoons powdered glucose
1 oz unflavored gelatin (4 envelopes)
⅔ cup strained fresh orange juice
Superfine sugar, for coating

1 Wet a pan approximately 8 inches square and a 1½ inch round cutter.
2 Mix the sugar, glucose and gelatin together in a heavy saucepan.
3 Stir in the orange juice using a wooden spoon.
4 Heat gently, stirring, until the sugar and gelatin have dissolved.
5 Pour into the wet pan and leave to set.
6 Dip the bottom of the pan briefly in hot water and turn the jelly out.
7 Cut into crescent shapes using the wet cutter.
8 Roll the jellies in superfine sugar to coat them evenly.
9 Store in an airtight container lined with waxed paper. Separate layers with waxed paper.

• LEMON SLICES •
Use ⅔ cup strained fresh lemon juice instead of orange juice.

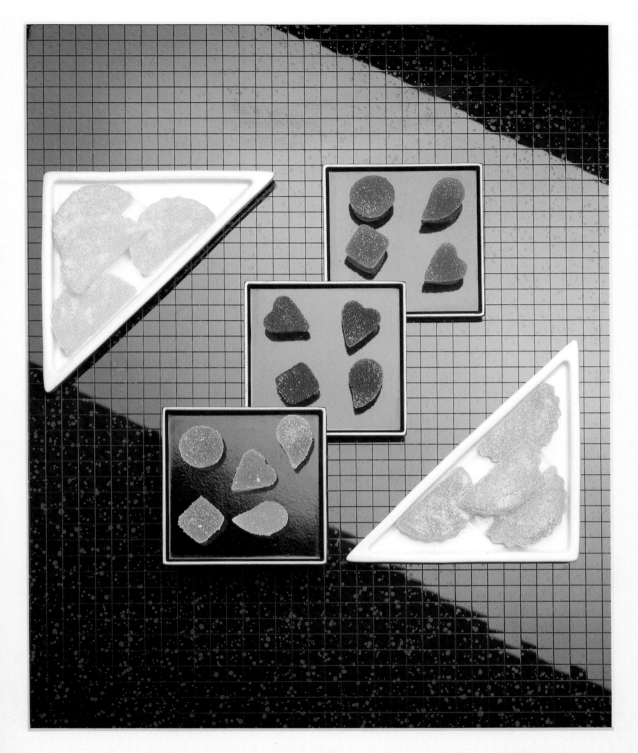

• ABOVE •
Orange Slices (top)
Fruit Jellies (center)
Lemon Slices (bottom)

C·R·E·M·E D·E M·E·N·T·H·E

MAKES ABOUT 1 lb
1 oz gum arabic
2 cups sugar
1 oz unflavored gelatin (4 envelopes)
½ cup cornstarch
A few drops of green food coloring
A few drops of peppermint oil
Sieved confectioners' sugar, for coating

1 Dampen a pan approximately 8 × 6 inches.
2 Dissolve the gum arabic in 4 tablespoons water.
3 Mix the sugar, gelatin and cornstarch together in a heavy saucepan, then blend in ⅔ cup water.
4 Add the gum arabic and heat gently, stirring with a wooden spoon until the sugar has dissolved.
5 Bring to a boil, stirring, and cook for 10 minutes, still stirring.
6 Remove from the heat and stir in coloring and peppermint oil.

7 Pour into the pan and leave to set.
8 Dip the bottom of the pan briefly in hot water then turn the jelly out.
9 Cut into squares and coat them in confectioners' sugar.
10 Store in an airtight container lined with waxed paper on a bed of confectioners' sugar. Separate layers with waxed paper.

R·A·S·P·B·E·R·R·Y J·U·J·U·B·E·S

MAKES ABOUT ½ lb
1 oz unflavored gelatin (4 envelopes)
½ cup sugar
1¼ cups sieved raspberry purée
Superfine sugar, for coating

1 Wet a pan approximately 6 inches square, and a cutter.
2 Mix the gelatin and sugar together in a heavy saucepan then stir in the raspberry purée and ⅔ cup water, using a wooden spoon.
3 Heat gently, stirring, until the sugar and gelatin have dissolved.
4 Bring to a boil and boil for 5 minutes.
5 Pour into the wet pan and leave to set.
6 Dip the bottom of the pan briefly in hot water, then turn the jelly out.
7 Cut into circles, crescents or fancy shapes using a suitable wetted cutter.
8 Roll the candies in superfine sugar to coat them evenly.

• BLACKCURRANT JUJUBES •
Use 1¼ cups sieved black currant purée instead of raspberry purée.

· ABOVE ·
Crème De Menthe
· OPPOSITE ·
Jujubes

• ABOVE •
Turkish Delight

T·U·R·K·I·S·H D·E·L·I·G·H·T
(traditional method)

MAKES ABOUT 1½ lb
2 cups sugar
¼ teaspoon tartaric acid
¾ cup cornstarch
1¾ cups confectioners' sugar, sifted
3 tablespoons clear honey
A few drops of lemon extract
A few drops of rose water
Red food coloring
For the coating
Approximately 1¾ cups confectioners' sugar, sifted

1 Butter or oil a pan approximately 12 × 4 inches.
2 Gently heat the sugar in ⅔ cup water in a heavy saucepan, stirring with a wooden spoon, until the sugar has dissolved.
3 Bring to a boil, cover and boil for 3 minutes.
4 Uncover and boil until the temperature reaches 240°F, the soft ball stage.
5 Add the tartaric acid and remove from the heat.
6 Blend the cornstarch and confectioners' sugar with ⅔ cup water in a heavy saucepan.
7 Bring 2½ cups water to a boil, then stir into the cornstarch/sugar paste. Bring to a boil, stirring, and beat vigorously until thick and opaque.
8 Lower the heat and gradually beat in the sugar syrup. Boil for 30 minutes until the mixture is a very pale straw color and transparent.
9 Beat in the honey, lemon extract, and rose water.
10 Pour half of the mixture into the pan. Add sufficient red food coloring to the remaining mixture to color it pale pink, then pour onto the mixture in the pan.
11 Leave until cold and set.
12 Cut into squares with a sharp knife dipped in confectioners' sugar. Toss the pieces in confectioners' sugar.

T·U·R·K·I·S·H D·E·L·I·G·H·T
(quick method)

MAKES ABOUT 1¼ lb
2 oz unflavored gelatin
2 cups sugar
¼ teaspoon citric acid
Rose water
Red food coloring
Scant ½ cup confectioners' sugar
¼ cup cornstarch

1 Pour 1¼ cups water into a heavy saucepan, sprinkle the gelatin over it, and leave to soften for 5 minutes.
2 Stir in the sugar and citric acid and heat gently until the sugar has dissolved, stirring with a wooden spoon.
3 Boil until the temperature reaches 240°F, soft ball stage.
4 Remove from the heat and leave to stand for 10 minutes.
5 Add the rose water to taste.
6 Pour half of the mixture into a pan approximately 8 × 6 inches. Add a few drops of food coloring to the remaining mixture, then pour that over the first mixture.
7 Leave in a cool place for 24 hours.
8 Sift the confectioners' sugar and cornstarch together, then sprinkle evenly over a sheet of waxed paper.
9 Turn the Turkish delight onto the paper and cut into squares with a sharp knife.
10 Toss the squares in the sugar mixture to coat them evenly.
11 Store in an airtight container between layers of waxed paper and keep in a cool place.

M·A·R·S·H·M·A·L·L·O·W·S

MAKES ABOUT 1 lb
• 2 cups sugar
• 1 tablespoon liquid glucose
• 1 oz unflavored gelatin (4 envelopes)
• 2 tablespoons orange flower water
• 2 egg whites
• Cornstarch and sieved confectioners' sugar, for dusting and coating
(For step-by-step illustrations, see page 27)

1 Lightly oil a pan approximately 8 inches square and dust it with a mixture of equal quantities of cornstarch and sieved confectioners' sugar.
2 Gently heat the sugar with the glucose and ⅞ cup water in a heavy saucepan, stirring with a wooden spoon, until the sugar has dissolved.
3 Bring to a boil, cover and boil for 3 minutes.
4 Uncover and boil until the temperature reaches 260°F, the hard ball stage.
5 Meanwhile, dissolve the gelatin in ½ cup water in a bowl placed over a saucepan of hot water.
6 Pour the gelatin into the syrup and add the orange flower water.
7 Whisk the egg whites until stiff.
8 Pour the syrup into the egg whites in a slow, thin, steady stream, whisking constantly.
9 Whisk until the mixture is thick and stiff.
10 Spread the mixture in the pan, using a metal spatula to smooth it out evenly, and leave to set.
11 Spread a work surface with cornstarch/confectioners' sugar mixture.
12 Run a small knife around the edges of the pan to loosen the mixture, then turn it out onto the surface.
13 Dust the top and sides with more cornstarch/confectioners' sugar mixture to coat them evenly.
14 Cut into circles using an oiled 1 inch cutter, or into squares by cutting first into 1 inch wide strips using an oiled large, sharp knife, then oiled scissors to form the squares.
15 Coat the sides of the shapes in cornstarch/confectioners' sugar mixture and leave to dry on a wire rack for 24 hours.
16 Store in an airtight container lined with waxed paper. Separate layers of marshmallows with waxed paper.

• ROSE MARSHMALLOWS •
Use rose water instead of orange flower water and add a few drops of pink food coloring, if liked.

• LEMON MARSHMALLOWS •
Use a few drops of lemon oil instead of orange flower water and add a few drops of yellow food coloring, if liked.

• PEPPERMINT MARSHMALLOWS •
Add a few drops of peppermint oil instead of orange flower water and add a few drops of green food coloring, if liked.

• COCONUT MARSHMALLOWS •
Coat the candies in shredded coconut instead of the cornstarch/confectioners' sugar mixture.

D·I·V·I·N·I·T·Y

MAKES ABOUT 1 lb
1¼ cups plus 1 tablespoon sugar
5 tablespoons light corn syrup
1 teaspoon vinegar
1 egg white
A few drops of vanilla extract
½ cup finely chopped nuts
¾ cup chopped mixed nuts

1 Gently heat the sugar, syrup and vinegar with ½ cup water in a heavy saucepan, stirring with a wooden spoon, until the sugar has dissolved and the syrup melted.
2 Bring to a boil, cover and cook for 3 minutes.
3 Uncover and boil until the temperature reaches 250°F, the hard ball stage.
4 Meanwhile whisk the egg white in a large bowl, set over a saucepan of just-simmering water, until it holds its shape.
5 Slowly pour the syrup into the egg white in a thin, steady stream, whisking constantly.
6 Stir in the vanilla extract and the nuts.
7 Beat until the mixture will hold its shape then drop small balls onto waxed paper.
8 Store in an airtight container and eat soon after making.

• ABOVE •
Marshmallows (top)
Divinity (bottom)

N·U·T·T·Y C·A·N·D·I·E·S

Nuts of all types are used in the making of all manner of candies. They may simply be coated in chocolate or fondant or they may be a vital ingredient as in crunchy praline, butter nut crunch or nut brittle. Any type of nut that is prepared in an identical way — chopped or ground, say — can be substituted for another in a recipe to lend a different nuance of flavor and texture. (For illustrations of preparing nuts, see page 39.)

P·R·A·L·I·N·E

MAKES ABOUT 1½ lb
1 lb nuts
2 cups sugar

1 Heat the oven to 350°F. Oil a marble slab or 2 large baking sheets.
2 Spread the nuts on a baking tray and place in the oven for 5 minutes to warm.
3 Gently heat the sugar in ⅔ cup water in a heavy saucepan, stirring with a wooden spoon, until the sugar has dissolved.
4 Bring to a boil, cover and boil for 3 minutes.
5 Uncover and boil until the syrup becomes a light caramel color and the temperature reaches 320°–338°F.
6 Dip the bottom of the saucepan in cold water immediately. Add the nuts and stir gently to coat them evenly with the syrup.

7 Pour onto the slab or sheets and leave to set.
8 Break into pieces and store in an airtight container in single layers between sheets of waxed paper.

B·U·T·T·E·R·E·D B·R·A·Z·I·L·S

MAKES ABOUT 1 lb
1⅓ cups soft light brown sugar
1 tablespoon powdered glucose
3 tablespoons unsalted butter, diced
1 cup shelled Brazil nuts, skinned
(other nuts can be used instead of Brazils)

1 Oil a marble slab or a large baking sheet.
2 Gently heat the sugar, glucose and butter in ⅔ cup water in a large saucepan, stirring with a wooden spoon, until the sugar has dissolved and the butter melted.
3 Bring to a boil, cover and boil for 3 minutes.
4 Uncover and boil until the temperature reaches 300°F, the hard crack stage.
5 Drop small spoonfuls onto the oiled slab or baking sheet, quickly place a nut in each circle and then, as quickly, spoon a little toffee over each nut.
　Keep the heat beneath the saucepan very low, and check the toffee constantly to make sure that a fairly constant temperature is maintained throughout and that the bottom does not burn.
6 Leave the coated Brazils to cool completely.
7 Wrap in waxed paper and store in an airtight container.

• ABOVE•
Buttered Brazils
•OPPOSITE•
Praline

• ABOVE •
Butter Nut Crunch
• OPPOSITE •
Sugared Almonds

S·U·G·A·R·E·D A·L·M·O·N·D·S

MAKES ABOUT 1½ lb
2 cups sugar
1½ cups almonds

1 Gently heat three-quarters of the sugar in generous ¼ cup water in a heavy saucepan, stirring with a wooden spoon, until the sugar has dissolved.

2 Bring to a boil, cover and boil for 3 minutes.

3 Uncover and boil until the temperature reaches 240°F, the soft ball stage.

4 Remove from the heat, add the almonds and stir with a wooden spoon until the syrup sets then looks powdery.

5 Turn the mixture into a colander placed over the saucepan.

6 When the sugar has drained through, stir in 2 tablespoons water, cover and bring to a boil.

7 Boil for 1 minute, then uncover and boil until the temperature reaches 240°F, the soft ball stage.

8 Remove from the heat, add the almonds and repeat steps 4 and 5.

9 Add the remaining sugar and 2 tablespoons water, cover and bring to a boil.

10 Boil for 1 minute then uncover and boil until the temperature reaches 240°F, the soft ball stage.

11 Repeat step 4.

12 Place the saucepan over the heat and heat, stirring constantly, until the sugar crystals on the side of the saucepan start to melt and the nuts look shiny.

13 Pour onto a marble surface or baking tray and immediately separate the nuts using a fork. Leave to set.

14 Store in an airtight jar.

B·U·T·T·E·R N·U·T C·R·U·N·C·H

MAKES ABOUT 1 lb
1½ cups sugar
1 tablespoon liquid glucose
1 cup unsalted butter, diced
1 cup nuts, toasted and chopped
A few drops of vanilla extract

1 Oil a pan approximately 7 inches square.

2 Gently heat the sugar, glucose and butter in ¼ cup water in a heavy saucepan, stirring with a wooden spoon, until the sugar has dissolved and the butter melted.

3 Bring to a boil, cover and boil for 3 minutes.

4 Uncover and boil until the temperature reaches 300°F, the hard crack stage.

5 Add the nuts and vanilla extract, pour into the pan and leave until beginning to set.

6 Mark into squares with a lightly oiled knife and leave to set completely.

7 Break into pieces, wrap in cellophane and store in an airtight container.

•ABOVE•
Sherry Walnuts
•OPPOSITE•
Honeyed Almonds

S·H·E·R·R·Y W·A·L·N·U·T·S

MAKES ABOUT 1 lb
1¼ cups sugar
½ cup sherry
A pinch of salt
½ teaspoon ground cinnamon
3 cups walnut halves

1 Oil a marble surface or large baking sheet.
2 Gently heat the sugar, sherry and salt in a heavy saucepan, stirring constantly with a wooden spoon, until the sugar has dissolved.
3 Bring to a boil, cover and boil for 3 minutes.
4 Uncover and boil until the temperature reaches 234°F, the soft ball stage.
5 Remove the pan from the heat then stir in the cinnamon and nuts. Beat vigorously until the mixture becomes cloudy.
6 Turn the mixture onto the surface or baking sheet and separate the nuts, using two lightly oiled forks. Leave to cool.
7 Store in an airtight container.

H·O·N·E·Y·E·D A·L·M·O·N·D·S

MAKES ABOUT 1 lb
1¼ cups sugar
¼ cup clear honey
2½ cups almonds
A few drops of vanilla extract

1 Oil a marble surface or a large baking sheet.
2 Gently heat the sugar and honey in ½ cup water in a heavy saucepan until the sugar has dissolved and the honey melted, stirring with a wooden spoon.
3 Bring to a boil, cover and boil until the temperature reaches 240°F, the soft ball stage.
4 Dip the base of the saucepan in cold water, then add the nuts and vanilla extract, and stir until the mixture is thick and creamy.
5 Pour onto the surface or sheet and separate the nuts, using two lightly oiled forks. Leave to cool.
6 Store in an airtight container between sheets of waxed paper.

N·U·T B·R·I·T·L·E

MAKES ABOUT 1½ lb
1½ cups sugar
⅔ cup light corn syrup
2 teaspoons powdered glucose
2 tablespoons unsalted butter, diced
2 cups coarsely chopped nuts, lightly toasted and warmed
1½ teaspoons baking soda

1 Oil a marble slab or wooden board.
2 Gently heat the sugar, syrup and glucose in ⅔ cup water in a heavy saucepan. Stir with a wooden spoon until the sugar has dissolved and the syrup melted.
3 Bring to a boil, cover and boil for 3 minutes.
4 Uncover and boil until the temperature reaches 300°F, the hard crack stage.
5 Add the butter and warm nuts.
6 Stir in the baking soda and pour the mixture onto the oiled surface in a thin layer. Spread the mixture out evenly using an oiled spatula.
7 As soon as it is cool enough to handle, gently stretch the mixture to a thin sheet with well oiled hands.

8 When completely cold, break it into pieces and store in an airtight container in single layers separated by sheets of waxed paper.

P·E·A·N·U·T B·R·I·T·L·E

MAKES ABOUT 1½ lb
1¼ cups plus 2 tablespoons sugar
¾ cup soft brown sugar
6 tablespoons unsalted butter, chopped
1 cup unsalted peanuts, chopped and slightly warmed

1 Butter or oil a pan 10 × 6 inches.
2 Gently heat the sugars and butter with ⅔ cup water in a heavy saucepan, stirring with a wooden spoon, until the sugar has dissolved and the butter melted.
3 Bring to a boil, cover and boil for about 3 minutes.
4 Uncover and boil until the temperature reaches 310°F, the hard crack stage.
5 Stir in the nuts, then slowly pour into the pan.
6 Leave to cool for 10 minutes until just beginning to set, then mark into fingers or squares with an oiled knife and leave to cool and set completely.
7 Break into fingers or squares and store in a cool place in an airtight container, between layers of waxed paper, for up to 2 weeks.

• ABOVE•
Peanut Brittle
• OPPOSITE•
Nut Brittle

C·R·Y·S·T·A·L·L·I·Z·E·D F·R·U·I·T·S A·N·D F·L·O·W·E·R·S

Crystallizing is really a method of preservation and is surely one of the most worthwhile. How else could you have pretty primroses glistening with sugar to add a natural touch of glamor and evoke memories of springtime in the depths of winter? As well as being delicious to eat on their own, crystallized and candied fruits transform ordinary puddings into mouthwatering desserts. (For illustrations of crystallizing method, see page 40.)

C·A·N·D·I·E·D F·R·U·I·T

MAKES ABOUT 1 lb
1 lb prepared fresh fruit (page 40)
Approximately 1½ lb sugar

1 Gently poach the fruit in sufficient water to cover until just tender: small or soft pieces will only take 2–4 minutes; larger, firmer ones such as apricots will need 10–15 minutes.
2 Transfer the fruit to a wire rack placed over a tray and leave to drain.
3 Measure 1¼ cups of the poaching liquid, add ¾ cup sugar and heat gently, stirring with a wooden spoon, until the sugar has dissolved. Bring to a boil.
4 Arrange the fruit in a single layer in a shallow dish and pour the boiling syrup over to cover the fruit completely. If there is insufficient syrup, prepare some more by dissolving 1 cup sugar in scant 1 cup water.
5 Cover the fruit with waxed paper to keep it completely submerged and leave in a warm place for 24 hours.
6 Using a perforated spoon or pancake turner, transfer the fruit to a wire rack placed over a tray and leave to drain.
7 Pour the soaking syrup into a saucepan, add ¼ cup sugar and heat gently, stirring with a wooden spoon, until the sugar has dissolved. Bring to a boil.
8 Return the fruit to the shallow dish, pour the syrup over, cover with waxed paper and leave in a warm place for 24 hours.
9 Repeat steps 6, 7 and 8 five times more.
10 Repeat step 6 then step 7 using 6 tablespoons sugar. Repeat step 8, but leave the fruit to soak for 48 hours instead of 24.
11 Repeat step 10 and leave for 4 days, or longer if you want very sweet fruit.
12 Using a perforated spoon or pancake turner, transfer the fruit to a wire rack placed over a tray and leave to drain.
13 Leave the fruit in a warm place, such as an airing cupboard or over a radiator, until completely dry.
14 Pack into cardboard or wooden boxes between layers of waxed paper, or use for crystallized or glacé fruits (page 40).

C·R·Y·S·T·A·L·L·I·Z·E·D F·R·U·I·T·S

MAKES ABOUT 1 lb
Superfine sugar
1 lb candied fruit (page 92)

1 Bring a saucepan of water to a boil and put plenty of superfine sugar into a bowl.
2 Spear one piece of fruit at a time on a dipping fork or a skewer, dip it in boiling water, allow the excess moisture to drain off, then roll the fruit in the sugar to coat it well and evenly, and pressing it in lightly.
3 Place the fruit on a wire rack and leave to dry in a warm place.

• ABOVE •
Candied Fruit
• OPPOSITE •
Crystallized Fruits

• ABOVE •
Candied Peel
• OPPOSITE •
Glacé Fruit

C·A·N·D·I·E·D P·E·E·L

TO CANDY ABOUT 5 SMALL ORANGES,
2 LEMONS OR 2 SMALL GRAPEFRUIT
1½ cups sugar

1 Scrub the fruit, cut it into halves or quarters and scrape away all the flesh.

2 Simmer the peel, just covered by water, for 1½–2 hours until tender, topping up with fresh water as necessary. Change the water two or three times when cooking grapefruit.

3 Remove the peel from the liquid with a perforated spoon or pancake turner and place on a wire rack placed over a tray to drain.

4 Measure 1¼ cups of the cooking liquor, adding extra water if necessary. Add 1 cup sugar and heat gently, stirring with a wooden spoon, until the sugar has dissolved.

5 Bring to a boil, add the peel, return to a boil, then cover and leave in a warm place for 2 days.

6 Using a perforated spoon or pancake turner, transfer the peel to a wire rack placed over a tray and allow to drain.

7 Add the remaining sugar to the syrup, heat gently, stirring with a wooden spoon, until the sugar has dissolved. Return the peel to the saucepan, bring to a boil, then simmer until the peel is transparent.

8 Leave the peel in the syrup for 2–3 weeks.

9 Using a perforated spoon or pancake turner, transfer the peel to a wire rack placed over a tray and leave to drain.

10 Leave in a warm place to dry completely, then store in airtight jars.

G·L·A·C·E F·R·U·I·T

MAKES ABOUT 1 lb
2 cups sugar
1 lb candied fruit (page 92)

1 Gently heat the sugar in ⅔ cup water, stirring with a wooden spoon, until the sugar has dissolved.

2 Bring to a boil and boil for 1 minute. Bring a saucepan of water to a boil.

3 Pour a little of the syrup into a cup. Cover the remaining syrup.

4 Spear one piece of fruit at a time on a dipping fork or skewer. Dip the fruit into the boiling water, allow the excess water to drain off then dip into the syrup in the cup.

5 Leave the fruit on a wire rack to drain.

6 As the syrup in the cup becomes cloudy, replace it with fresh syrup from the saucepan.

7 Turn the pieces of fruit over occasionally so they dry evenly.

M·A·R·R·O·N·S G·L·A·C·E·S

MAKES ABOUT 1½ lb
1 lb peeled chestnuts
2 cups sugar
2 tablespoons liquid glucose

1 Simmer the chestnuts in sufficient water to cover until a needle can be inserted into the base quite easily – about 40 minutes.
2 Gently heat the sugar and glucose in ½ cup water in a heavy saucepan, stirring with a wooden spoon until the sugar has dissolved.
3 Bring to a boil and boil to 215°F.
4 Drain the chestnuts well, put into a heatproof bowl and pour the syrup over. Leave for 24 hours.
5 Place the bowl over a saucepan of boiling water and gradually heat until the temperature reaches boiling point. Remove the nuts using a perforated spoon, allowing excess syrup to drain back into the bowl, and heat the syrup to 216°F.
6 Return the nuts to the syrup, remove the pan from the heat and leave for 12 hours.

7 Repeat steps 5 and 6, heating the syrup to 220°F, 223°F, then finally 227°F.
8 Using a perforated spoon, transfer the chestnuts to a wire rack placed over a tray and leave to drain.
9 Leave to dry in a warm place such as an airing cupboard before wrapping individually in cellophane.

C·R·Y·S·T·A·L·L·I·Z·E·D F·L·O·W·E·R·S

MAKES COATING FOR PETALS FROM 2 FLOWERS
1 teaspoon gum arabic
2 teaspoons rose water
Food coloring
Flower petals free from blemishes
1 cup superfine sugar

1 Dissolve the gum arabic in the rose water.
2 Pour a little of the solution into a saucer and add a few drops of appropriate food coloring.
3 Using a soft paint brush or small make-up brush, completely coat three or four petals at a time with the gum arabic solution.
4 Dip the petals in the sugar, then sift more sugar over them.
5 Repeat with the remaining petals.
6 Place the coated petals on a wire rack and leave in a warm place to dry and become brittle, turning them over occasionally so that they dry evenly.
7 Store in an airtight container on tissue paper, paper tissues or absorbent kitchen paper.

• ABOVE•
Crystallized Flowers
• OPPOSITE•
Marrons Glacés

F·U·D·G·E

According to the dictionary, 'fudge' is nonsense! But to the serious candy-eater, fudge is quite the reverse – a delicacy to be savored and deliberated over. How could anything that can contain such deliciously diverse ingredients as cream, buttermilk, carob, rum, ginger, raisins and peanuts bound with the sweet taste of honey, or the exotic darkness of brown sugar, be nonsense? (For illustration of method, see page 20.)

V·A·N·I·L·L·A F·U·D·G·E
(with evaporated milk)

MAKES ABOUT 1¼ lb
2 cups granulated sugar
¼ cup unsalted butter, diced
⅔ cup evaporated milk
⅔ cup milk
A few drops of vanilla extract

1 Butter or oil a pan approximately 7 inches square.
2 Gently heat the sugar, butter and milks in a heavy saucepan, stirring with a wooden spoon, until the sugar has dissolved and the butter melted.
3 Bring to a boil, cover and boil for 3 minutes.
4 Uncover and boil until the temperature reaches 240°F, the soft ball stage, stirring occasionally.
5 Place the saucepan on a cold surface, add the vanilla extract then beat with a wooden spoon until the mixture becomes stiff and paler in color.
6 Pour into the pan and leave until beginning to set.
7 Mark into squares with a lightly oiled knife and leave to cool completely.
8 Cut or break into pieces. Store in a cool place in an airtight container between layers of waxed paper.

• MARSHMALLOW FUDGE •
Add 8 oz marshmallows, chopped
Proceed as above, adding the marshmallows at stage 5 before the beating.

• RAISIN FUDGE •
Add ½ cup raisins, chopped
Proceed as above, adding the raisins at stage 5 before the beating.

• GINGER FUDGE •
Add ½ cup preserved ginger, chopped
Proceed as above, adding the ginger at stage 5 before the beating.

C·O·F·F·E·E F·U·D·G·E
(made in a microwave oven)

MAKES ABOUT 1 lb
• ¼ cup unsalted butter, diced
• ⅔ cup evaporated milk
• ⅔ cup milk
2 cups sugar
2 tablespoons coffee extract

1 Oil a pan approximately 6 inches square.
2 Heat the butter and milks in a large bowl on 100 per cent (full) power for 3½ minutes until the butter has melted.
3 Stir in the sugar then heat on 100 per cent (full) power for 1–2 minutes until the sugar has completely dissolved.
4 Heat for 15 minutes, stirring every 2 minutes, until the temperature reaches 240°F, the soft ball stage.
5 Place the bowl on a cold surface, add the coffee extract then beat thoroughly until the mixture becomes thick and paler in color.
6 Pour immediately into the pan and leave until just beginning to set.
7 Mark into squares with a lightly oiled knife and leave to set completely.
8 Break into pieces and store in an airtight container between layers of waxed paper.

• ABOVE •
Vanilla Marshmallow Fudge (top)
Coffee Fudge (bottom)

C·H·O·C·O·L·A·T·E F·U·D·G·E

MAKES ABOUT 1½ lb
2 cups sugar
⅔ cup milk
½ cup plus 2 tablespoons butter, chopped
⅔ cup semisweet chocolate pieces
3 tablespoons clear honey
A few drops of vanilla extract

1 Butter or oil a pan approximately 7 inches square.
2 Gently heat the sugar in the milk in a heavy saucepan, stirring with a wooden spoon, until the sugar has melted.
3 Add the butter, chocolate and honey and stir until melted.
4 Bring to a boil. Cover and boil for 3 minutes.
5 Uncover and boil until the temperature reaches 240°F, the soft ball stage.
6 Remove from the heat, plunge the base of the saucepan in cold water until the mixture is lukewarm.
7 Beat the mixture very well until it becomes thick, creamy and paler in color.
8 Pour the mixture into the pan and leave until beginning to set, then mark into squares with a lightly oiled knife. Leave to set.

9 Break or cut into pieces then store in an airtight container between layers of waxed paper.

• FRUIT AND NUT FUDGE •
Add ½ cup chopped nuts
⅓ cup seedless raisins
Adding the fruit and nuts before step 7.

• MARSHMALLOW FUDGE •
Add 8 oz marshmallows, chopped
Adding the marshmallows before step 7.

• CHERRY CHOCOLATE FUDGE •
Add ⅓ cup glacé cherries, chopped
Proceed as above, adding the cherries before step 7.

G·I·N·G·E·R A·N·D H·O·N·E·Y F·U·D·G·E

MAKES ABOUT 1¼ lb
1½ cups sugar
¼ cup clear honey
¼ cup unsalted butter, diced
⅔ cup milk
A few drops of ginger extract
¾ cup stem ginger, well drained and finely chopped

1 Butter or oil a pan approximately 7 × 5 inches.
2 Gently heat the sugar, honey, butter and milk in a heavy saucepan, stirring with a wooden spoon, until the sugar has dissolved and the honey melted.
3 Bring to a boil. Cover and boil for 3 minutes.
4 Uncover and boil until the temperature reaches the 240°F, the soft ball stage.
5 Dip the bottom of the saucepan in cold water, add the ginger extract and beat until the mixture becomes thick and paler in color.
6 Pour into the pan and cool until just beginning to set.
7 Mark into squares with a lightly oiled knife and leave to set completely.
8 Cut or break into pieces and store between layers of waxed paper in an airtight container.

• ABOVE •
Cherry Chocolate Fudge
• OPPOSITE •
Ginger and Honey Fudge

• ABOVE •
Carob-Raisin Fudge (top)
Tablet (center)
Buttermilk and Honey Fudge (bottom)

C·A·R·O·B-R·A·I·S·I·N F·U·D·G·E

MAKES ABOUT 1½ lb
2⅔ cups Barbados sugar
¾ cup milk
2 tablespoons unsalted butter, diced
6 oz plain carob, finely chopped
1 cup raisins

1 Butter or oil a pan approximately 8 inches square.
2 Gently heat the sugar, milk, butter, carob and ⅔ cup water in a heavy saucepan, stirring with a wooden spoon, until the sugar has dissolved and the butter and carob melted.
3 Bring to a boil, cover and boil for 3 minutes.
4 Uncover and boil until the temperature reaches 240°F, the soft ball stage.
5 Stand the saucepan in cold water until it begins to cool. Stir in the raisins and leave to cool.
6 Beat with a wooden spoon until the mixture thickens and becomes lighter in color.
7 Pour into the pan and leave until just beginning to set.
8 Mark into squares with a lightly oiled knife and leave to set completely.
9 Cut or break into squares then store in an airtight container between layers of waxed paper. Keep in a cool place.

T·A·B·L·E·T

MAKES ABOUT 1¼ lb
2 cups brown granulated sugar
3¼ cups light cream
A few drops of vanilla extract

1 Oil a pan approximately 6 inches square.
2 Gently heat the sugar with the cream and ¼ cup water in a heavy saucepan, stirring with a wooden spoon, until the sugar has dissolved.
3 Bring to a boil, cover and boil for 3 minutes.
4 Uncover and boil until the temperature reaches 245°F, the firm ball stage.

5 Add the vanilla extract, allow to cool slightly, then beat with a wooden spoon until the mixture becomes paler in color but is still liquid.
6 Pour into the pan and leave until beginning to set.
7 Mark into squares with a lightly oiled knife and leave to set completely.
8 Break into pieces and store in a cool place in an airtight container between layers of waxed paper.

B·U·T·T·E·R·M·I·L·K A·N·D H·O·N·E·Y F·U·D·G·E

MAKES ABOUT 1 lb
2⅔ cups soft light brown sugar
1 teaspoon baking powder
1 cup buttermilk
3 tablespoons clear honey

1 Oil a pan approximately 7 inches square.
2 Mix the sugar and baking powder together in a heavy saucepan then stir in the buttermilk and honey. Heat gently, stirring with a wooden spoon, until the sugar has dissolved and the honey melted.
3 Bring to a boil, cover and boil for 3 minutes.
4 Uncover and boil until the temperature reaches 238°F, soft ball stage, stirring occasionally.
5 Remove from the heat, plunge the saucepan in cold water and leave until the temperature has reached 110°F.
6 Beat until the mixture becomes thick and paler.
7 Pour into the pan and leave until beginning to set.
8 Mark into squares with a lightly oiled knife and leave to set completely.
9 Break into pieces and store in a cool place in an airtight container between layers of waxed paper.

· NUTTY BUTTERMILK AND HONEY FUDGE ·
Add ¾ cup chopped walnuts, hazelnuts, almonds or Brazils.
Prepare the fudge as above, adding the nuts at the beginning of step 6.

O·R·A·N·G·E F·U·D·G·E

MAKES ABOUT 1¼ lb
2 cups sugar
⅔ cup evaporated milk
¼ cup butter, diced
2 tablespoons finely grated orange rind
2 tablespoons orange juice

1 Butter or oil a pan approximately 7 inches square.
2 Gently heat the sugar, evaporated milk and butter in a heavy saucepan, stirring with a wooden spoon, until the sugar has dissolved and the butter melted.
3 Add the orange rind and juice.
4 Bring the mixture to a boil. Cover and boil for 3 minutes.
5 Uncover and boil until the temperature reaches 240°F, the soft ball stage, stirring frequently.
6 Remove the saucepan from the heat and immediately plunge the base into cold water.
7 Beat the mixture vigorously until it is thick and creamy.
8 Pour the fudge into the pan and leave until almost cold.
9 Mark into squares with a lightly oiled knife and leave until firm.
10 Cut into pieces with a sharp knife and store in an airtight container between layers of waxed paper.

D·A·R·K C·R·E·A·M F·U·D·G·E

MAKES ABOUT ¾ lb
2 cups soft dark brown sugar
½ cup heavy cream
½ teaspoon baking soda
½ tablespoon unsalted butter
A few drops of vanilla extract

1 Butter or oil a pan approximately 7 inches square.
2 Gently heat the sugar with the cream, baking soda and 2 tablespoons water in a heavy saucepan, stirring with a wooden spoon, until the sugar has dissolved.

3 Bring to a boil, cover and boil for 3 minutes.
4 Uncover and boil until the temperature reaches the medium-soft ball stage, 237°F.
5 Remove from the heat and beat in the butter and vanilla extract.
6 Cool slightly then beat until the mixture becomes thick and paler in color.
7 Turn into the pan and leave until just beginning to set.
8 Cut into squares with a lightly oiled knife and leave to cool completely.
9 Break into pieces and store in a cool place in an airtight container between layers of waxed paper.

P·E·N·U·C·H·E

MAKES ABOUT 1 lb
• 2⅔ cups light soft brown sugar
• ¾ cup milk or light cream
1 tablespoon unsalted butter
• 1 tablespoon light corn syrup
A few drops of vanilla extract

1 Butter or oil a pan approximately 7 inches square.
2 Gently heat the sugar, milk, butter and syrup in a heavy saucepan, stirring with a wooden spoon, until the sugar has dissolved and the butter and syrup melted.
3 Bring to a boil, cover and boil for 3 minutes.
4 Uncover and boil until the temperature reaches 234°F, the soft ball stage.
5 Stand the saucepan in cold water until the temperature reaches about 110°F.
6 Add the vanilla extract and beat with a wooden spoon until the mixture becomes thick and paler in color.
7 Pour into the pan and leave until beginning to set.
8 Mark into squares with a lightly oiled knife and leave to set completely.
9 Break or cut into squares. Store in a cool place, in an airtight container between layers of waxed paper, for 2–3 weeks.

· ABOVE ·
Orange Fudge, Dark Cream Fudge, Penuche

P·E·A·N·U·T B·U·T·T·E·R F·U·D·G·E

MAKES ABOUT 1 lb
2½ cups sugar
¾ cup milk or cream
2 tablespoons corn syrup
¼ cup peanut butter
A few drops of vanilla extract

1 Oil a pan approximately 8 inches square.
2 Gently heat the sugar, milk or cream and syrup in a heavy saucepan, stirring with a wooden spoon, until the sugar has dissolved and the syrup melted.
3 Bring to a boil, cover and boil for 2–3 minutes.
4 Uncover and boil until the temperature reaches the 234°F, the soft ball stage.

5 Stand the saucepan in cold water until the temperature of the syrup reaches 110°F.
6 Beat in the peanut butter and vanilla extract and beat until the mixture thickens and becomes paler in color.
7 Pour into the pan and leave until just set.
8 Mark into squares and leave to set completely.
9 Cut or break into pieces, wrap in waxed paper, and store in an airtight container in a cool place for up to 2 weeks.

• ABOVE •
Peanut Butter Fudge
Fudge (with sour cream) (right)
• OPPOSITE •
Maple Fudge

F·U·D·G·E
(with sour cream)

MAKES ABOUT 1¼ lb
2 cups sugar
½ cup sour cream
¼ cup milk
1 tablespoon light corn syrup
2 tablespoons unsalted butter, diced
A few drops of vanilla extract
1 cup chopped mixed nuts
⅓ cup seedless raisins

1 Butter or oil a pan approximately 8 inches square.
2 Gently heat the sugar, sour cream, milk, and syrup in a heavy saucepan until the sugar has dissolved, stirring with a wooden spoon.
3 Bring to a boil. Cover and boil for 3 minutes.
4 Uncover and boil until the temperature reaches 237°F, the soft ball stage.
5 Dip the bottom of the saucepan in cold water. Add the butter and leave to cool for 1 hour.
6 Add the vanilla extract and beat with a wooden spoon until the mixture becomes thick and paler in color.
7 Add the nuts and raisins and pour into the pan.
8 Leave until beginning to set then mark into squares using a lightly oiled knife. Leave to set completely.
9 Cut or break into pieces then store in an airtight container between layers of waxed paper.

M·A·P·L·E F·U·D·G·E

MAKES ABOUT 1¼ lb
2 cups sugar
½ cup maple syrup
1 cup milk
1 tablespoon liquid glucose
2 tablespoons unsalted butter, diced
A few drops of vanilla extract

1 Oil a pan approximately 7 inches square.
2 Gently heat the sugar, with the maple syrup, milk, and liquid glucose in a heavy saucepan, stirring with a wooden spoon, until the sugar has dissolved.
3 Bring to a boil, cover and boil for 3 minutes.
4 Uncover and boil until the temperature reaches 238°F, the soft ball stage.
5 Remove from the heat immediately and swirl in the butter.
6 Place the saucepan on a cold surface and leave until the mixture cools to 110°F.
7 Add vanilla extract and beat until the mixture becomes thick and paler in color.
8 Pour into the pan and cool until just beginning to set.
9 Mark into squares with a lightly oiled knife and leave to set completely.
10 Cut or break into pieces then store in an airtight container between layers of waxed paper.

R·U·M A·N·D R·A·I·S·I·N F·U·D·G·E

MAKES ABOUT 1 lb

⅞ cup brown granulated sugar
⅞ cup sugar
¼ cup unsalted butter, diced
⅔ cup light cream
1 tablespoon dark rum
⅓ cup seedless raisins

1 Butter or oil a pan approximately 9 inches square.
2 Gently heat the sugars, butter and cream in a heavy saucepan until the sugars have dissolved and the butter melted, stirring with a wooden spoon.
3 Add the rum and bring to a boil. Cover and boil for 3 minutes.

4 Uncover and boil until the temperature reaches 240°F, the soft ball stage.
5 Plunge the bottom of the saucepan immediately into cold water.
6 Cool for 5 minutes, then beat vigorously with a wooden spoon until the mixture is thick, creamy and pale in color.
7 Stir in the raisins.
8 Pour into the pan and leave until almost cold.
9 Mark into squares with a lightly oiled knife and leave until firm.
10 Cut into pieces and store in a cool place in an airtight container between layers of waxed paper.

O·P·E·R·A F·U·D·G·E

MAKES ABOUT 1 lb

1¾ cups sugar
1 cup heavy cream
A few drops of vanilla extract

1 Oil a pan approximately 8 inches square.
2 Gently heat the sugar and cream in a heavy saucepan, stirring with a wooden spoon, until the sugar has dissolved.
3 Bring to a boil, cover and boil for 3 minutes.
4 Uncover and boil until the temperature reaches 234°F, the soft ball stage.
5 Dip the bottom of the saucepan in cold water and leave to cool to 110°F.
6 Add the vanilla extract and beat until the mixture becomes thick and creamy in color.
7 Pour into the pan, cover with a damp cloth and leave for 30 minutes.
8 Uncover and leave until just set. Mark into squares with a lightly oiled knife and leave to set completely.
9 Cut or break into pieces and store in an airtight container between layers of waxed paper.

• ABOVE •
Opera Fudge
• OPPOSITE •
Rum and Raisin Fudge

C·A·R·A·M·E·L·S

Smooth, velvety and chewy, caramels may be soft or they may have a firmer 'bite' depending on the temperature to which the syrup is boiled. The most luxurious caramels contain cream but less rich candies can be made with milk, unsalted butter, condensed or evaporated milk. Variety can be added by the inclusion of nuts or dried fruits, and by varying the type of sugar used. They can also be given a coating of chocolate.

C·R·E·A·M C·A·R·A·M·E·L·S

MAKES ABOUT ¾ lb
1⅓ cups light soft brown sugar
6 tablespoons unsalted butter
½ cup light cream
A few drops of vanilla extract

1 Oil a pan approximately 6 inches square.
2 Gently heat the sugar with the butter, cream and 1 tablespoon water in a heavy saucepan, stirring with a wooden spoon, until the sugar has dissolved and the butter melted.
3 Bring to a boil, cover and boil for 3 minutes.
4 Uncover and boil until the temperature reaches 250°F, the hard ball stage, but do not stir.
5 Pour into the pan and leave until just beginning to set.

6 Mark into squares with a lightly oiled knife and leave to set completely.
7 Break into pieces, wrap in waxed paper and store in an airtight container wrapped individually in waxed paper.

B·U·T·T·E·R·S·C·O·T·C·H C·R·E·A·M C·A·R·A·M·E·L·S

MAKES ABOUT 1¼ lb
2 cups brown granulated sugar
½ cup unsalted butter, diced
⅔ cup heavy cream
A few drops of vanilla extract

1 Butter or oil an 8 inch pan.
2 Gently heat the sugar, butter and cream in ⅔ cup water in a heavy saucepan, stirring with a wooden spoon, until the sugar has dissolved and the butter melted.
3 Bring to a boil, cover and boil for 3 minutes.
4 Uncover and boil until the temperature reaches 310°F, the hard crack stage.
5 Stir in the vanilla extract and remove from the heat.
6 Pour into the pan and leave until just beginning to set.
7 Mark into squares with a lightly oiled knife and leave to set completely.
8 Break into pieces, wrap in waxed paper and store in an airtight container.

• ABOVE •
Cream Caramels
• OPPOSITE •
Butterscotch Cream Caramels

• ABOVE •
Chocolate - coated Cream Caramels
• OPPOSITE •
Golden Caramels

C·H·O·C·O·L·A·T·E-C·O·A·T·E·D C·R·E·A·M C·A·R·A·M·E·L·S

MAKES ABOUT 2 lb
2 cups sugar
1 cup powdered glucose
2/3 cup heavy cream
2 tablespoons butter, chopped
1 lb semisweet chocolate, chopped

1 Butter or oil a pan approximately 7 inches square.
2 Gently heat the sugar in 2/3 cup water in a heavy saucepan, stirring with a wooden spoon, until the sugar has dissolved.
3 Add the glucose and bring to a boil. Cover and boil for 3 minutes.
4 Uncover and boil until the temperature reaches 240°F, the soft ball stage.
5 Meanwhile, gently warm the cream and butter in a small saucepan over a low heat.
6 Add to the syrup and boil gently until the temperature reaches 250°F.
7 Pour into the pan and leave to cool.
8 When firm enough to handle turn the caramel onto a board, and cut into 1/2 inch square pieces with lightly oiled scissors. Once cut the squares will spread slightly.
9 Melt the chocolate in a bowl placed over a saucepan of hot water. Remove from the heat and cool to about 85°F.
10 Using a chocolate dipping fork, a carving fork or similar wide-pronged fork, dip one caramel at a time into the chocolate to coat it completely. Allow excess chocolate to drain off and place the coated caramel on waxed paper.
11 Repeat until all the caramels have been coated. Keep the chocolate at the right temperature by placing it over hot water or removing it as necessary.
12 Leave the caramels to harden, then leave for another 2–3 days before eating.

G·O·L·D·E·N C·A·R·A·M·E·L·S

MAKES 3/4 lb
1 cup sugar
1/2 cup powdered glucose
2 tablespoons light corn syrup
6 tablespoons milk
A pinch of salt
A few drops of vanilla extract

1 Oil a pan approximately 6 × 8 inches.
2 Gently heat the sugar, glucose, syrup, milk and salt in a heavy saucepan, stirring with a wooden spoon, until the sugar has dissolved.
3 Bring to a boil, cover and boil for 3 minutes.
4 Uncover and boil slowly until the temperature reaches 255°F, the hard ball stage.
5 Remove the saucepan from the heat, plunge the bottom in cold water, then stir in a little vanilla extract.
6 Pour the mixture into the pan. Leave to cool.
7 Mark into squares with a lightly oiled knife and leave to cool.
8 Break into pieces and store in an airtight container, wrapped individually in waxed paper.

•ABOVE•
Vanilla Caramels (top right)
Honey and Hazelnut Caramels (center)
Rich Butterscotch Caramels (top left)

R·I·C·H B·U·T·T·E·R·S·C·O·T·C·H C·A·R·A·M·E·L·S

MAKES ABOUT 1¼ lb

2 cups brown granulated sugar
½ cup unsalted butter, diced
⅔ cup heavy cream
A few drops of vanilla extract

1 Oil a pan approximately 7 inches square.
2 Gently heat the sugar, butter and cream with ⅔ cup water in a heavy saucepan, stirring with a wooden spoon, until the sugar has dissolved and the butter melted.
3 Bring to a boil, cover and boil for 3 minutes.
4 Uncover and boil until the temperature reaches 280°F, the soft crack stage.
5 Add the vanilla extract.
6 Pour into the pan and leave until just beginning to set.
7 Mark into squares with an oiled knife and leave to set completely.
8 Break into pieces and store in an airtight container wrapped individually in waxed paper.

H·O·N·E·Y A·N·D H·A·Z·E·L·N·U·T C·A·R·A·M·E·L·S

MAKES ABOUT 1 lb

½ cup clear honey
generous ½ cup light corn syrup
6 tablespoons unsalted butter, diced
1 cup chopped hazelnuts

1 Oil a pan approximately 6 inches square.
2 Gently heat the honey, syrup and butter in a heavy saucepan, stirring with a wooden spoon, until they have melted.
3 Bring to a boil, cover and boil for 3 minutes.
4 Uncover and boil until the temperature reaches 265°F, the hard ball stage.
5 Remove from the heat and add the nuts.

6 Pour into the pan and leave until just beginning to set.
7 Mark into squares with an oiled knife and leave to set.
8 Break into pieces, wrap individually in waxed paper, and store in an airtight container.

V·A·N·I·L·L·A C·A·R·A·M·E·L·S

MAKES ABOUT 1½ lb

2 cups sugar
⅔ cup milk
8 tablespoons liquid glucose
1 small can condensed milk
¼ cup unsalted butter, diced
A few drops of vanilla extract

1 Oil a pan approximately 7 inches square.
2 Gently heat the sugar in the milk in a heavy saucepan, stirring with a wooden spoon until the sugar has dissolved.
3 Cover, bring to a boil and boil for 3 minutes.
4 Uncover, add the glucose and boil until the temperature reaches 250°F, the hard ball stage.
5 Slowly stir in the condensed milk then the butter.
6 Boil until the temperature reaches 255°F, the hard ball stage.
7 Add the vanilla extract and pour into the pan.
8 Leave until just beginning to set, then mark into squares with a lightly oiled knife.
9 Leave to set, then break into pieces and store in an airtight container, wrapped individually in waxed paper.

M·A·R·Z·I·P·A·N

There are two types of marzipan – cooked and uncooked. Both can be flavored and colored easily but the first, based on a boiled sugar syrup, is the easier to 'work' and mold, so is really the one to use for decorative and novelty candies. Traditionally marzipan is made from ground almonds, but other ground nuts, such as the simple yet delectable hazelnut, can be substituted to make enjoyably different variations.

U·N·C·O·O·K·E·D M·A·R·Z·I·P·A·N

MAKES ABOUT 1 lb

scant 1 cup confectioners' sugar, sieved
½ cup superfine sugar
2 cups ground almonds
1 teaspoon lemon juice
2 egg yolks, beaten

1 Mix the sugars together.
2 Stir in the ground almonds.
3 Add the lemon juice and sufficient egg yolk to give a stiff consistency.
4 Form into a ball and knead lightly until smooth.
5 Use as required or wrap in waxed paper and store in an airtight container in a cool place.

B·O·I·L·E·D M·A·R·Z·I·P·A·N

MAKES ABOUT 2 lb

2 cups sugar
A pinch of cream of tartar
4 cups ground almonds
2 egg whites, lightly beaten
Confectioners' sugar for dusting

1 Sprinkle confectioners' sugar over a marble surface or a large baking sheet.
2 Gently heat the sugar in ⅔ cup water in a heavy saucepan, stirring with a wooden spoon until the sugar has dissolved.
3 Add the cream of tartar and bring to a boil. Cover and boil for 3 minutes.
4 Uncover, and boil until the temperature reaches 240°F, the soft ball stage.
5 Dip the bottom of the saucepan in cold water, then beat until the syrup becomes thick and creamy.
6 Stir in the ground almonds, then the egg whites.
7 Place the saucepan over a low heat and stir thoroughly for about 2 minutes until the mixture thickens.
8 Turn the marzipan onto the surface or sheet and begin to work it with a metal spatula until it is cold enough to handle, then knead it with hands lightly dusted with confectioners' sugar until it is smooth and pliable.
9 Use as required or wrap in waxed paper, place in an airtight container, and store in a cool place.

C·H·O·C·O·L·A·T·E M·A·R·Z·I·P·A·N

MAKES ABOUT ¾ lb
6 tablespoons superfine sugar
Scant ¾ cup confectioners' sugar, sieved
1½ cups ground almonds
⅓ cup semisweet chocolate pieces, finely chopped
1 egg yolk
1 teaspoon lemon juice
A few drops of vanilla extract
Extra superfine sugar for coating

1 Stir the sugars together then stir in the ground almonds.
2 Melt the chocolate with 1 tablespoon hot water in a bowl placed over a saucepan of hot water.
3 Stir the chocolate into the ground almond mixture.
4 Mix the egg yolk, lemon juice and vanilla extract together, add to the chocolate mixture and knead well, adding a little extra lemon juice if the mixture is too stiff.
5 Form into small balls then roll them in superfine sugar to give them a coating.
6 Leave to dry. Place in small paper candy cases and pack loosely in an airtight container. Store in a cool place.

• ABOVE •
Chocolate Marzipan

S·I·M·P·L·E I·D·E·A·S U·S·I·N·G M·A·R·Z·I·P·A·N

• STUFFED DATES •

1 Select good quality dessert dates.

2 With a small sharp knife slit along the length of each date and carefully lift out the pit.

3 Add a few drops of food coloring to some marzipan, then form it into small pieces that will fit into the cavities left by the pits.

4 Fill the dates with the marzipan, roll them in superfine sugar then put in small paper candy cases. Leave to dry.

• STUFFED PLUMS, APRICOTS, PRUNES AND GRAPES •

1 These can all be prepared in the same way as stuffed dates, but dried apricots and prunes must be soaked and cooked first until just tender, then drained well (unless they are the type that requires no soaking).

• STUFFED WALNUTS •

1 Form some colored marzipan into thick discs then sandwich between 2 walnut halves.

2 Place in small paper candy cases.

• CARAMEL-COATED STUFFED WALNUTS •

1 Stuffed nuts can be dipped into a light caramel syrup (page 19) to coat them then left on waxed paper to dry before being placed in small paper candy cases.

• MARZIPAN LOGS •

1 Form colored marzipan into a long sausage.

2 Roll contrasting colored marzipan to a rectangle of the same length as the sausage and wide enough to wrap around it.

3 Brush the rectangle with lightly beaten egg white, place the sausage on top and wrap the rectangle around, pressing it gently but firmly in place.

4 Cut into lengths using a sharp knife, then brush or spread with melted semisweet chocolate and make a bark effect on the surface. Leave to set.

• MARZIPAN FRUITS AND FLOWERS •

1 Form the shapes from small pieces of plain, boiled marzipan, then use a small paint-brush and food colorings to color, tint and shade them as appropriate.

2 For citrus fruit, give the typical finish by rolling the fruit lightly on a nutmeg or fine grater. Stud with a clove to resemble the stem.

3 For strawberries, raspberries and other berries, lightly roll over a nutmeg or fine grater then roll in superfine sugar.

4 For apples and pears, form a stem from a clove, a piece of angelica or strip of liquorice. Paint a small dot of brown coloring on the other side.

• ABOVE •
Fondant Fruits
• OPPOSITE •
Stuffed Walnuts and Apricots

• ABOVE •
Chequerboard (top right)
Harlequin Marzipan (bottom left)
Neapolitan Slices (top left)
• OPPOSITE •
Neapolitan Slices

S·O·P·H·I·S·T·I·C·A·T·E·D I·D·E·A·S U·S·I·N·G M·A·R·Z·I·P·A·N

• MARZIPAN CHEQUERBOARD •

See page 42 for step-by-step illustrations

1 Divide a piece of marzipan in half and knead a few drops of food coloring into one piece.

2 Roll out each piece separately on a work surface lightly sprinkled with confectioners' sugar to a rectangle about ¼ inch thick.

3 Brush one piece with lightly beaten egg white, then lay the second piece on top. Pass a rolling pin lightly over the top to gently press the pieces together.

4 Trim the edges of the rectangle with a sharp knife then cut it lengthways into 3 strips of equal width.

5 Brush the top of one strip lightly with lightly beaten egg white and place another strip on top, making sure that it is completely lined up. Repeat with the remaining strip.

6 Pass a rolling pin over the stack to press the pieces together.

7 With a long, sharp knife cut the stack lengthways into 4 strips.

8 Lay one strip flat, brush with egg white and place a second strip on the first, turning it over so the colors are reversed. Brush with egg white and repeat with the remaining strips, making sure the colors always alternate.

9 Pass the rolling pin lightly over the stack.

10 Cut into slices using a sharp knife then leave to dry on waxed paper for a few hours.

• HARLEQUIN MARZIPAN •

1 Color 3 or 4 pieces of marzipan, all the same size, with a few drops of contrasting food colors.

2 On a surface lightly dusted with confectioners' sugar roll each piece out separately to rectangles of the same size about ¼ inch thick.

3 Brush the top of one piece lightly with lightly beaten egg white, lay another on top and pass the rolling pin lightly over to press them together gently.

4 Brush the top lightly with egg white and repeat with the remaining pieces.

5 Trim the edges using a large, sharp knife then cut into pieces.

6 Coat the pieces in superfine sugar, pressing it in gently, then leave for several hours to dry.

• NEAPOLITAN MARZIPAN SLICES •

1 Knead a few drops of 2 contrasting food colorings – red and green, for instance – into 2 equal sized pieces of marzipan.

2 Color a third piece of the same size yellow.

3 On a surface lightly dusted with confectioners' sugar roll the 2 colored pieces of marzipan separately into strips ½ inch thick and about 1 inch wide.

4 Cut each strip in half lengthways using a sharp knife and trim them so all the pieces are exactly the same size.

5 Roll the yellow piece of marzipan out very thinly to the same length as the strips and about 4½ inches wide. Brush with lightly beaten egg white.

6 Place 2 strips of different colors along the plain strip, brush the tops with beaten egg white, then place the other 2 strips on top of them so the colors are reversed.

7 Wrap the plain marzipan around the strips to resemble a Battenburg cake, gently pressing all the pieces of marzipan together.

8 Cut into slices using a sharp knife.

P·I·N·E·A·P·P·L·E M·A·R·Z·I·P·A·N R·O·L·L

MAKES ABOUT 1¾ lb

10 oz boiled marzipan (page 116)
A few drops of coffee extract
5 oz green colored marzipan
Lightly beaten egg white
½ cup glacé pineapple pieces (page 95)
⅔ cup semisweet chocolate pieces, melted (page 34)
Approximately 1 cup shredded coconut

1 Divide the marzipan in half and work the coffee extract into one half.
2 Roll out the plain, coffee-flavored and green marzipan separately into thin strips about 2½ inches wide.
3 Brush the coffee-flavored strip lightly with beaten egg white, place the green strip on top, and pass the rolling pin over the surface lightly to press them together.

4 Brush the green strip lightly with beaten egg white, place the plain strip on top and pass the rolling pin over the surface lightly to press the strips together. Trim the edges with a long, sharp knife.
5 Lay pieces of glacé pineapple along the length of the strip, then roll the strip up along the long edge like a jelly roll, pressing it gently but firmly into shape.
6 Brush or spread the roll with melted chocolate, working in one direction only, then coat with shredded coconut.
7 Leave to set then cut into slices.

• CHERRY MARZIPAN ROLL •
Use brandied cherries instead of glacé pineapple.

M·A·R·Z·I·P·A·N M·U·S·H·R·O·O·M·S

MAKES ABOUT 18

1 tablespoon unsweetened cocoa powder
8 oz boiled marzipan (page 116)

1 Dissolve the cocoa powder in 2 teaspoons hot water.
2 Work the cocoa liquid into half of the marzipan.
3 Form small pieces of the uncolored marzipan into shapes resembling mushroom caps.
4 Form the colored marzipan into mushroom stems, and small discs to fit on the underside of the caps.
5 Press the discs in place and mark lightly with prongs of a fork to resemble the gills.
6 Fix the stems in place.

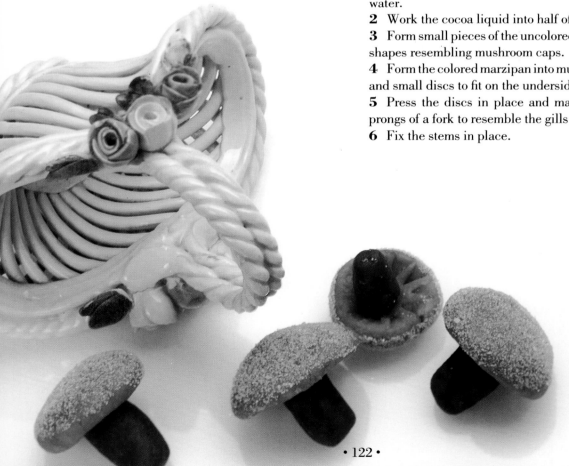

• ABOVE •
Pineapple Marzipan Roll
• OPPOSITE •
Marzipan Mushrooms

B·O·I·L·E·D C·A·N·D·I·E·S

The category of boiled or perhaps crunched candies includes traditional candies that are sucked rather than chewed – favorites like lollipops, spiral barley sugars, two-tone mint humbugs.

Lollipops are the easiest to make, then barley sugars then humbugs, so try the first two to gain a little experience before attempting the latter. And allow yourself plenty of uninterrupted time as they take a while to prepare. Humbugs can be the most sociable of candies to make as well as the most exhausting, and you'll be grateful for an extra pair of arms to help you with the 'pulling' (see page 30 for illustrations of method.)

C·L·E·A·R M·I·N·T·S

MAKES ABOUT 1¼ lb
• 2 cups sugar
Scant 1 cup powdered glucose
½ teaspoon peppermint extract
A few drops of green coloring (optional)

1 Lightly oil a shallow pan approximately 11 × 7 inches.
2 Gently heat the sugar with ¾ cup water in a heavy saucepan, stirring with a wooden spoon until the sugar has dissolved.
3 Stir in the glucose, increase the heat and bring to a boil. Cover and boil for 3 minutes.
4 Uncover and boil, gradually reducing the heat under the saucepan, until the temperature of the syrup reaches 300°F, the soft crack stage.
5 Remove the saucepan from the heat, then stir in the peppermint extract and the coloring, if used.
6 Pour the syrup into the pan and leave to cool until firm enough to handle.
7 Using a metal spatula, turn the mint out of the pan then, with oiled kitchen scissors and working quickly, cut the mint into squares before it hardens.
8 Leave to harden, then wrap individually in cellophane and store in an airtight container.

P·E·A·R D·R·O·P·S

MAKES ABOUT 1¼ lb
2 cups sugar
Scant 1 cup powdered glucose
1 teaspoon cream of tartar
A few drops of pear extract
Confectioners' sugar, for coating

1 Oil a pan approximately 7 inches square.
2 Gently heat the sugar, glucose and ¾ cup water in a heavy saucepan, stirring with a wooden spoon, until the sugar has dissolved.
3 Bring to a boil, cover and boil for 3 minutes.
4 Uncover and boil until the temperature reaches 310°F, the hard crack stage.
5 Add the cream of tartar and pear extract, and pour the syrup into the pan.
6 Leave for a short while until just cool enough to handle, then very quickly cut off small pieces using lightly oiled scissors and form into small balls.
7 Coat in confectioners' sugar then wrap in cellophane paper. Store in an airtight container.

• ABOVE •
Clear Mints (top)
Pear Drops (bottom)

L·O·L·L·I·P·O·P·S

2 cups sugar
1 tablespoon powdered glucose
3 or 4 flavorings and appropriate food colorings
(eg, orange oil and orange coloring, raspberry
flavoring and red coloring, lemon oil and yellow
coloring, peppermint oil and green coloring)
Lollipop sticks

1 Oil a marble surface or large baking sheet.
2 Gently heat the sugar and glucose in ⅔ cup water in a heavy saucepan, stirring with a wooden spoon, until the sugar has dissolved.
3 Pour into a measuring jug and measure off one-third or one-quarter, depending on whether 3 or 4 flavorings are being used.
4 Add the chosen coloring to the measured-off amount, bring to a boil, cover and boil for 3 minutes.
5 Uncover and boil until the temperature reaches 265°F, the hard ball stage. Remove from the heat and add the appropriate flavoring.
6 Drop small, round pools of the syrup onto the oiled surface using a dessert or soup spoon. Lay a lollipop stick in each pool. Add a little more syrup, if necessary, to cover the sticks.
7 Leave to harden then carefully remove from the surface and wrap individually in cellophane paper.
8 Repeat with the remaining syrup in batches, using different colorings and flavorings.

B·A·R·L·E·Y S·U·G·A·R T·W·I·S·T·S

MAKES ABOUT 1 lb
2 tablespoons pearl barley
Thinly pared rind and juice of ½ lemon
2 cups sugar
¼ teaspoon cream of tartar

1 Put the barley into a saucepan. Stir in 1¼ cups cold water and bring to a boil.
2 Drain the barley and rinse it under cold running water.
3 Return the barley to the rinsed saucepan, stir in 3¾ cups cold water and the lemon rind. Bring to a boil, reduce the heat, cover and simmer for about 1½–1¾ hours until the barley is soft.
4 Strain off the liquid, add the lemon juice and make up to 2½ cups with cold water.
5 Lightly oil a marble surface or baking sheet.
6 Gently heat the sugar, cream of tartar and barley water in a heavy saucepan, stirring constantly with a wooden spoon, until the sugar has dissolved.
7 Bring to a boil, cover and boil for 3 minutes.
8 Uncover and boil until the temperature reaches 310°F, the hard crack stage.
9 Pour the syrup onto the surface or baking sheet so that it spreads out to an even shallow pool.
10 Leave the barley sugar to cool until it firms around the edges.
11 Using a lightly oiled metal spatula, ease one edge of the sheet of syrup away from the surface or baking sheet, then pull the edge up with your hands and fold it over the middle of the sheet of syrup, laying it down evenly so that there are no wrinkles.
12 Immediately fold the opposite edge over to meet the first edge in the middle.
13 Gently lift the folded sheet using the oiled metal spatula and, cutting alternately from opposite sides of the sheet, cut it into strips about ½ inch wide with oiled scissors. Twist each strip into a spiral as it is cut.
14 Leave the strips to harden then wrap individually in cellophane and store in an airtight container.

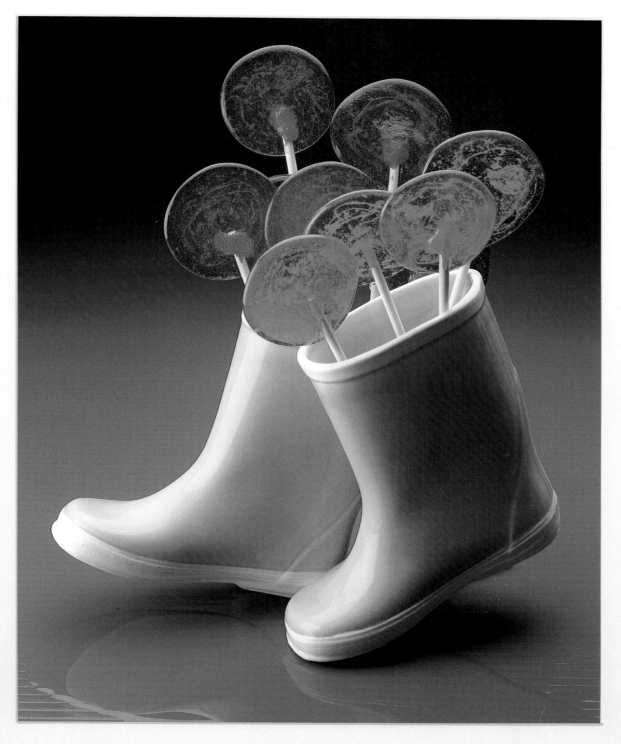

• ABOVE•
Lollipops
• OPPOSITE•
Barley Sugar Twists

H·U·M·B·U·G·S

MAKES ABOUT 1 lb
2 cups sugar
1 tablespoon liquid glucose
¼ teaspoon cream of tartar

1 Oil a marble slab or baking sheet.
2 Gently heat the sugar, liquid glucose and ⅔ cup water in a heavy saucepan, stirring with a wooden spoon until the sugar has dissolved.
3 Add the cream of tartar, bring to a boil, cover and boil for 3 minutes.
4 Uncover and boil until the temperature reaches 290°F, the soft crack stage.
5 Pour the syrup into two pools on the oiled surface.
6 As the syrup cools lift the edges with an oiled metal scraper or metal spatula and fold them into the center.
7 With oiled hands form one pool into a roll, then pull and twist the roll until it becomes opaque, much paler in color and has a satin finish. Fold over twice lengthways to form 4 strands, then twist these together, pulling gently, to make a long rope.
8 Form the remaining syrup into a roll, then pull it into a rope of the same length as the first piece.
9 Lay the two pieces side by side, twist them together, then fold the length that is formed over and over to make a short rope.
10 Gently but firmly and quickly, and giving a twist, pull along the length of the rope.
11 Using lightly oiled scissors cut into small pieces, giving the rope a half turn towards you so the pieces have a triangular surface.
12 Store in an airtight container between layers of waxed paper.

• MINT HUMBUGS •

Add a few drops of peppermint extract at the soft crack stage.

E·D·I·N·B·U·R·G·H R·O·C·K

MAKES ABOUT 1 lb
2 cups sugar
1 teaspoon liquid glucose
¼ teaspoon cream of tartar
Flavoring and food coloring
(eg, raspberry flavoring or rose water
and pink food coloring)

1 Oil a marble slab or baking sheet.
2 Gently heat the sugar, glucose and 1¼ cups water in a heavy saucepan, stirring with a wooden spoon, until the sugar has dissolved.
3 Add the cream of tartar, bring to a boil, cover and boil for 3 minutes.
4 Uncover and boil until the temperature reaches 275°F, the soft crack stage.
5 Remove from the heat, quickly add flavoring and coloring and pour onto the surface.
6 As the edges cool lift them up using an oiled metal scraper or metal spatula, and fold them in to the center.
7 As soon as it is cool enough to handle, lift the syrup using an oiled scraper and pull into a roll with lightly oiled hands.
8 Pull into a long thin rope, fold in half and pull again. Continue to pull and fold for as long as the rope is supple, which should be about 20 minutes.
9 Cut into lengths using lightly oiled scissors and leave in a warm place for 24 hours so the rock becomes powdery and soft.
10 Store in an airtight container between layers of waxed paper, or wrap individually in cellophane or waxed paper.

• ABOVE •
Edinburgh Rock (top)
Humbugs (bottom)

N·O·U·G·A·T

It hardly takes a Latin scholar to deduce that the word 'nougat' is derived from the Latin for 'nut'. But could it be that it takes a plentiful supply of that compact source of good ingredients (nuts, honey and egg whites) to make a Latin scholar? Perhaps not, but it would certainly make the learning of that dead language far more pleasurable! (For illustration of method, see page 32.)

N·O·U·G·A·T

MAKES ABOUT 1¼lb
Rice paper
¼ cup clear honey
1½ cups sugar
2oz liquid glucose
3 egg whites
¼ cup glacé cherries, chopped
2 tablespoons candied angelica, chopped
1 cup almonds, chopped

1 Line a pan, approximately 12 × 4 inches or 7 inch square, with rice paper.
2 Melt the honey in a bowl over a saucepan of hot water.
3 Gently heat the sugar in ⅔ cup water in a heavy saucepan, stirring with a wooden spoon, until the sugar has dissolved.
4 Add the glucose and bring to a boil. Cover and boil for 3 minutes.
5 Uncover and boil until the temperature reaches 280°F, the soft crack stage.
6 Pour the honey into the syrup and boil until the temperature reaches 290°F.
7 Dip the bottom of the saucepan in cold water.
8 Whisk the egg whites stiffly, then pour in the syrup in a slow, then steady, stream, whisking constantly.
9 Place over a pan of hot water and whisk until the mixture becomes firm.
10 Remove from the heat and stir in the fruits and nuts.
11 Pour into the pan and cover with rice paper. Place a board on top, then put some weights on, and leave overnight.
12 Turn the nougat out of the pan, trim away excess rice paper and cut the nougat into squares or fingers. Wrap individually and store in an airtight container.

• ABOVE •
Nougat

N·O·U·G·A·T W·I·T·H W·H·I·T·E C·H·O·C·O·L·A·T·E

MAKES ABOUT 2 lb
Rice paper
1¾ cups sugar
½ cup clear honey
2 egg whites
½ cup good quality white chocolate pieces, melted
scant 1 cup almonds, toasted
1 cup hazelnuts, toasted
½ cup pistachio nuts
⅓ cup glacé cherries, halved

1 Line a pan approximately 8 inches square with rice paper.
2 Gently heat the sugar in ½ cup water in a heavy saucepan, stirring with a wooden spoon, until the sugar has dissolved.
3 Cover the saucepan and bring to a boil.
4 Uncover and boil until the temperature reaches 302°F, the hard crack stage.
5 Meanwhile, melt the honey in a bowl placed over a saucepan of hot water and continue to heat until the temperature reaches 120°F.
6 Whisk the egg whites in a large bowl until very stiff, then pour in the syrup in a very slow, steady stream, whisking constantly.
7 Pour in the honey in the same way, whisking constantly.
8 Place the bowl over a saucepan of hot water and whisk until the mixture is very thick and firm.
9 Remove from the heat, stir in the melted chocolate, then fold in the warmed nuts and the cherries.
10 Transfer to the pan, spread it out evenly with an oiled metal spatula and cover with rice paper. Place a board on top and place heavy weights on the board. Leave overnight.
11 Turn the nougat out of the pan, trim away the excess rice paper, and cut the nougat into squares or fingers using a sharp knife. Wrap in cellophane and store in an airtight container.

C·H·O·C·O·L·A·T·E A·N·D H·A·Z·E·L·N·U·T N·O·U·G·A·T

MAKES ABOUT 1½ lb
Rice paper
2 cups sugar
¼ cup unsalted butter, diced
scant 1 cup powdered glucose
2 egg whites
⅓ cup semisweet chocolate pieces
¾ cup hazelnuts, toasted and chopped

1 Line the inside of a pan approximately 8 × 6 inches with rice paper.
2 Gently heat the sugar and butter in ⅔ cup water in a heavy saucepan, stirring with a wooden spoon, until the sugar has dissolved and the butter melted.
3 Add the glucose and bring to a boil. Cover and boil for 3 minutes.
4 Uncover and boil until the temperature reaches 270°F, the soft crack stage.
5 Meanwhile, whisk the egg whites stiffly in a bowl.
6 Gradually pour the syrup into the egg whites in a slow, thin, steady stream, whisking constantly
7 Place the bowl over a saucepan of boiling water and heat until the temperature reaches 250°F, the hard ball stage, whisking constantly.
8 Meanwhile, melt the chocolate in a bowl placed over a saucepan of hot water.
9 Remove the egg white and syrup mixture from the heat and beat in the chocolate. Add the nuts and pour into the pan, cover with rice paper, then put some weights on top and leave overnight.
10 Turn the nougat out of the pan, trim away excess rice paper, and cut the nougat into squares or fingers.
11 Wrap individually and store in an airtight container.

• ABOVE •
Nougat with White Chocolate (top)
Chocolate and Hazelnut Nougat (bottom)

T·O·F·F·E·E·S

Toffees can come in a variety of flavors, depending upon the type of sugar used for the syrup. Although always hard, toffees can vary too in the degree of hardness or brittleness; the higher the temperature to which the syrup is boiled the more brittle the toffee, hence the category of toffees known as 'brittles'. But whether your taste is for hard or super-hard, mono- or multi-colored, light and creamy or rich and dark flavored toffees, the following recipes will give you plenty of scope and choice.

O·L·D-F·A·S·H·I·O·N·E·D T·O·F·F·E·E

MAKES ABOUT 1 lb
2 cups brown granulated sugar
4 tablespoons vinegar

1 Oil a pan approximately 6 inches square.
2 Gently heat the sugar with the vinegar and generous 1 cup water in a heavy saucepan, stirring with a wooden spoon until the sugar has dissolved.
3 Bring to a boil, cover and boil for 3 minutes.
4 Uncover and boil until the temperature reaches 285°F, the soft crack stage.
5 Pour into the pan and leave until just beginning to set.

6 Mark into squares with a lightly oiled knife. Leave to set completely.
7 Break into pieces and store in an airtight container wrapped individually in waxed paper.

H·O·N·E·Y A·N·D L·E·M·O·N T·O·F·F·E·E

MAKES ABOUT 1¼ lb
1/3 cup clear honey
2 cups brown granulated sugar
3/4 cup unsalted butter, diced
1 tablespoon lemon juice

1 Butter or oil a pan approximately 8 inches square.
2 Gently heat all the ingredients in a heavy saucepan, stirring with a wooden spoon, until the sugar has dissolved and the butter melted.
3 Bring to a boil, cover and boil for 3 minutes.
4 Uncover and boil until the temperature reaches 290°F, the soft crack stage.
5 Pour immediately into the pan and leave until just beginning to set.
6 Mark into squares with a lightly oiled knife and leave to set completely.
7 Break or cut into pieces. Wrap the pieces individually in waxed paper, twisting the ends together, and store in an airtight container.

• ABOVE •
Honey and Lemon Toffee
• OPPOSITE •
Old-Fashioned Toffee

M·O·L·A·S·S·E·S T·A·F·F·Y

MAKES ABOUT 1 lb
1 cup molasses
⅞ cup sugar
2 teaspoons vinegar
¼ cup unsalted butter, diced

1 Oil a marble slab or large baking sheet.
2 Gently heat the molasses, sugar and vinegar in a heavy saucepan, stirring with a wooden spoon, until the molasses has melted and the sugar dissolved.
3 Cover and bring to a boil.
4 Uncover and boil until the temperature reaches 244°F, the firm ball stage.
5 Add the pieces of butter and boil slowly to 266°F, the hard ball stage.
6 Pour the syrup onto the slab or baking sheet.
7 As soon as the edges are cool enough to handle, fold them over towards the center with oiled fingers. Pull the sheet of taffy out, stretch it, then fold it back on itself again. Repeat this movement rhythmically until it begins to resemble a crystal ribbon, then start twisting it as well as folding and pulling it.

8 When it becomes opaque and very firm form it into a long rope and cut into small pieces using oiled scissors or an oiled sharp knife.
9 Put the pieces on waxed paper and leave to harden.
10 Wrap individually in waxed paper and store in an airtight container.

T·R·E·A·C·L·E T·O·F·F·E·E

MAKES ABOUT 1¼ lb
2⅔ cups soft dark brown sugar
⅔ cup sweetened condensed milk
6 tablespoons butter, diced
1 tablespoon vinegar
⅓ cup molasses
⅓ cup light corn syrup

1 Butter or oil a pan approximately 11 × 7 inches.
2 Dissolve the sugar in the condensed milk over a low heat, stirring constantly.
3 Add the remaining ingredients and stir until melted.
4 Bring to a boil, cover and boil for 3 minutes.
5 Uncover and boil until the temperature reaches 270°F, the soft crack stage.
6 Pour the mixture into the pan and leave to cool for 5 minutes.
7 Mark into squares with an oiled knife and leave to set.
8 Break into squares when cold and store in an airtight container individually wrapped in cellophane.

• ABOVE •
Treacle Toffee
• OPPOSITE •
Molasses Taffy

H·O·N·E·Y·C·O·M·B T·O·F·F·E·E

MAKES ABOUT 1 lb
2 cups sugar
4 tablespoons vinegar
3 tablespoons light corn syrup
½ teaspoon baking soda, free from lumps

1 Butter or oil a pan approximately 8 inches square.
2 Gently heat the sugar, vinegar and syrup with 1¼ cups water in a heavy saucepan, stirring with a wooden spoon until the sugar has dissolved and the syrup melted.
3 Bring to a boil, cover and boil for 3 minutes.
4 Uncover and boil until the temperature reaches 285°F, the soft crack stage.
5 Remove from the heat and stir in the baking soda, mixing well to allow the bubbles to subside a little.

6 Pour into the pan and leave until just beginning to set.
7 Mark into squares with a lightly oiled knife. Leave to set completely.
8 Cut or break into pieces. Wrap individually in waxed paper, twisting the ends together, and store in an airtight container.

H·O·N·E·Y·C·O·M·B

(made in a microwave oven)

MAKES ABOUT ½ lb
1 cup sugar
1 tablespoon light corn syrup
¼ teaspoon cream of tartar
- ½ teaspoon baking soda

1 Oil a pan approximately 7 inches square.
2 Heat ⅔ cup water in a large bowl on 100 per cent (full) power for 2 minutes.
3 Stir in the sugar, syrup and cream of tartar, heat for 1 minute at 100 per cent then stir until the sugar has dissolved.
4 Heat for 10 minutes on 100 per cent (full) power until the temperature reaches 310°F, the hard crack stage.
5 Just before the syrup is ready blend the soda with 1 teaspoon hot water.
6 Stir the baking soda liquid into the syrup then quickly pour into the pan and leave until just beginning to set.
7 Mark into squares with an oiled knife and leave to set completely.
8 Break into pieces and store in an airtight container wrapped individually in cellophane paper.

• ABOVE •
Honeycomb Toffee
• OPPOSITE •
Honeycomb Toffee
(made in a microwave oven)

B·U·T·T·E·R·S·C·O·T·C·H

MAKES ABOUT 1 lb
2 cups brown granulated sugar
¼ cup unsalted butter, diced

1 Butter a pan approximately 7 × 5 inches.
2 Gently heat the sugar and butter in ⅔ cup water in a heavy based saucepan, stirring with a wooden spoon, until the sugar has dissolved and the butter melted.
3 Bring to a boil, cover and boil for 3 minutes.
4 Uncover and boil until the temperature reaches 280°F, the soft crack stage.
5 Pour into the pan and leave until just beginning to set.
6 Mark into squares with a lightly oiled knife and leave to set completely.
7 Break into pieces, wrap in waxed paper and store in an airtight container.

B·U·T·T·E·R·S·C·O·T·C·H

(made in a microwave oven)

MAKES ABOUT 1 lb
2 cups sugar
¼ teaspoon cream of tartar
6 tablespoons unsalted butter, diced
A few drops of vanilla extract

1 Oil a pan approximately 11 × 7 inches.
2 Heat ⅔ cup water in a large bowl on 100 per cent (full) power for 1½ minutes.
3 Stir in the sugar and heat on 100 per cent (full) power for 4 minutes, stirring every minute, until the sugar has dissolved.
4 Add the cream of tartar and heat on 100 per cent (full) power for 8 minutes until the temperature reaches 240°F.
5 Add the butter and heat for a further 5 minutes to 280°F, without stirring.
6 Add the vanilla extract, pour into the pan and leave until just beginning to set.
7 Mark into squares with an oiled knife and leave to set completely.
8 Break into squares and store in an airtight container wrapped individually in cellophane.

• ABOVE •
Butterscotch
• OPPOSITE •
Butterscotch (made in a microwave oven)

B·R·A·Z·I·L N·U·T T·O·F·F·E·E C·U·S·H·I·O·N·S

MAKES ABOUT 1 lb
2 cups brown granulated sugar
2 tablespoons light corn syrup
2 tablespoons unsalted butter, diced
½ teaspoon cream of tartar
1 tablespoon vinegar
¾ cup Brazil nuts, chopped (other nuts can be used instead of Brazils)

1 Lightly oil a marble or wooden surface.
2 Gently heat the sugar and syrup in ⅔ cup water in a heavy saucepan, stirring with a wooden spoon until the sugar has dissolved and the syrup melted.
3 Bring to a boil, cover and boil for 1 minute.
4 Add the butter, cream of tartar and vinegar. Cover and boil for 3 minutes.
5 Uncover and boil until the temperature reaches 300°F, the hard crack stage.
6 Pour onto the oiled surface and sprinkle the nuts over.
7 Using an oiled metal spatula, fold the sides of the toffee sheet over the nuts, and continue doing this until just cool enough to handle.
8 With oiled fingers form the sheet into a roll, then stretch it into a long sausage. Fold the sausage in half and pull it again into a sausage. Repeat until it begins to harden.
9 Fold the long sausage in half and twist the two halves together, then repeat the folding and twisting for as long as the sausage remains supple – about 20 minutes.
10 Fold the sausage in half then in half again, twist all four strands together and pull into a long thin rope.
11 Cut into small pieces using oiled scissors. Wrap individually in cellophane or waxed paper and store in an airtight container.

S·O·F·T C·R·E·A·M M·O·L·A·S·S·E·S T·O·F·F·E·E

MAKES ABOUT 1¼ lb
1 cup sugar
• ¼ cup unsalted butter, diced
1 cup molasses
½ cup heavy cream
½ cup light cream
• Scant ½ cup walnuts, chopped

1 Place small paper candy cases on a baking sheet.
2 Gently heat the sugar, butter and molasses in the creams in a heavy saucepan until the sugar has dissolved and the butter and molasses have melted. Stir with a wooden spoon continuously.
3 Bring to a boil over a low heat, then cover and boil for 3 minutes.
4 Uncover and boil until the temperature reaches 250°F, the firm ball stage.
5 Add the nuts, pour into the paper cases and leave to set.
6 Store in an airtight container with waxed paper separating the layers.

• ABOVE •
Soft Cream Molasses Toffee
• OPPOSITE •
Brazil Nut Toffee Cushions

H·A·Z·E·L·N·U·T T·O·F·F·E·E

MAKES ABOUT 1¼ lb

½ cup shelled hazelnuts, roughly chopped
1 cup sugar
1⅓ cups soft light brown sugar
3 tablespoons unsalted butter, diced
2 teaspoons vinegar
A few drops of vanilla extract

1 Oil a pan approximately 7 inches square.
2 Spread the nuts out on a baking tray and warm gently in a very low oven.
3 Gently heat the sugars, butter and vinegar in ⅔ cup water in a heavy saucepan, stirring with a wooden spoon, until the sugars have dissolved and the butter melted.
4 Bring to a boil, cover and boil for 3 minutes.
5 Uncover and boil until the temperature reaches 300°F, the hard crack stage.
6 Add vanilla extract and pour half into the pan.
7 Scatter the nuts over the surface, then pour the remaining toffee over.

8 Leave until just beginning to set then mark into squares with a lightly oiled knife. Leave to set completely.
9 Break into squares and store in an airtight container wrapped individually in cellophane paper.

E·V·E·R·T·O·N T·O·F·F·E·E

MAKES ABOUT 1¾ lb

½ cup butter, chopped
1½ cups brown granulated sugar
generous ½ cup molasses
generous ½ cup light corn syrup

1 Oil a pan approximately 8 inches square.
2 Gently heat the butter, sugar, molasses and syrup in a heavy saucepan until the sugar has dissolved and the molasses melted, stirring with a wooden spoon.
3 Bring to a boil, cover and boil for 3 minutes.
4 Uncover and boil until the temperature reaches 290°F, the soft crack stage.
5 Plunge the bottom of the saucepan in cold water immediately.
6 Pour the toffee into the pan and leave until beginning to set.
7 Mark the toffee into squares using a lightly oiled knife and leave to set completely.
8 Break or cut into squares and store in an airtight container, wrapped individually in cellophane paper.

• ABOVE •
Hazelnut Toffee
• OPPOSITE •
Everton Toffee

F·O·N·D·A·N·T

Meltingly smooth 'creamy' fondant is extremely versatile. It can be flavored in innumerable ways during its preparation or small amounts can be flavored separately. It also has many uses, as it can be rolled out and cut into shapes, can be coated in chocolate, melted and poured into molds, or used as a coating. As true fondant requires some expertise, inexperienced cooks will find the uncooked fondant more useful. (For illustrations of methods, see page 22.)

F·O·N·D·A·N·T
(uncooked)

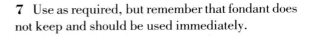

MAKES ABOUT 1 lb
3½ cups confectioners' sugar, sieved
3 tablespoons liquid glucose
1 egg white, lightly whisked
Flavoring and coloring (optional)

1 Lightly dust a work surface with extra confectioners' sugar.
2 Mix the confectioners' sugar and glucose together and add sufficient egg white to give a stiff but pliable mixture.
3 Turn onto the surface and knead very well until smooth and feeling slightly moist.
4 Form the fondant into a ball then flatten it out using a rolling pin.
5 Make a series of slits across the surface and put the flavoring and coloring into the slits.
6 Knead the fondant again to distribute the ingredients evenly.

7 Use as required, but remember that fondant does not keep and should be used immediately.

• ORANGE CREAMS •
Add a few drops of orange oil and orange food coloring.
1 Shape into small balls, then rub them lightly on a fine grater so the surface resembles orange peel.
2 Place a very small piece of angelica on the top of each to resemble the stem.
3 Leave in a cool place for 24 hours to dry.

C·R·E·A·M
F·O·N·D·A·N·T
(uncooked)

MAKES ABOUT 1 lb
3½ cups confectioners' sugar
½ teaspoon cream of tartar
3 tablespoons heavy cream, whipped
1 small egg white, lightly whisked

1 Dust a work surface with extra sieved confectioners' sugar.
2 Sieve the confectioners' sugar and cream of tartar together.
3 Mix in the cream and sufficient whisked egg white to give a firm but pliable mixture.
4 Knead for 5 minutes on the work surface.
5 Roll out with a rolling pin dusted with confectioners' sugar to about ½–¾ inch thick and cut into shapes with a cutter lightly coated with confectioners' sugar.

• ABOVE •
Uncooked Cream Fondant
• OPPOSITE •
Orange Creams

• ABOVE •
Walnut Coffee Creams (top)
Coffee Creams (right)
Maraschino Creams (center)
Peppermint Creams (left)
• OPPOSITE •
Vanilla Creams

F·O·N·D·A·N·T

MAKES ABOUT ¾ lb

2 cups sugar
1 tablespoon liquid glucose
Confectioners' sugar, for dusting
Coloring and flavoring (see below)

1 Sprinkle a marble slab or large baking sheet with cold water.

2 Gently heat the sugar with the glucose and ⅔ cup water in a heavy saucepan, stirring with a wooden spoon, until the sugar has dissolved.

3 Bring to a boil and boil for 3 minutes.

4 Uncover and boil until the temperature reaches 240°F, the soft ball stage.

5 Quickly dip the bottom of the saucepan into cold water.

6 Quickly pour the syrup onto the slab or baking sheet and leave to cool for a few minutes.

7 Using a dampened metal scraper or large metal spatula, lift the edges of the syrup and fold them into the center until the mixture is glossy and viscous and has a faint yellow color.

8 Using a dampened wooden spatula work the mixture in a continuous figure of eight action for 5-10 minutes, until it becomes white and crumbly and stirring is extremely difficult.

9 With lightly moistened hands knead the fondant for 5–10 minutes until it feels moist and is free of lumps. Use a moistened metal scraper or metal spatula to lift the fondant if it sticks to the surface.

10 Form the fondant into a ball, put it on a lightly moistened plate, cover with a damp cloth and leave in a cool place for 12 hours to ripen.

11 Dust the work surface with confectioners' sugar, place the ball of fondant in the confectioners' sugar and press it out flat.

12 Make a series of deep slits in the fondant and put the coloring and flavoring into the slits.

13 Knead the fondant well to mix the flavoring and coloring evenly.

14 Use as required.

15 Store fondant candies in an airtight container in single layers separated by sheets of waxed paper.

• PEPPERMINT CREAMS •

1 Add a few drops of peppermint oil to the basic fondant mixture.

2 Roll the fondant out to about ¼ inch thick on a surface dusted with confectioners' sugar and using a rolling pin that has been coated with confectioners' sugar.

3 Cut into circles with a 1 inch cutter dusted with confectioners' sugar.

4 Put into paper cases and leave to dry.

• COFFEE CREAMS •

1 Add a few drops of coffee extract or very strong black coffee to the basic fondant mixture.

2 Form into small balls or shape as for peppermint creams.

• WALNUT COFFEE CREAMS •

1 Shape coffee-flavored fondant (as above) into balls about 1 inch in diameter.

2 Flatten slightly then press a walnut half on top of each.

• VANILLA CREAMS •

1 Add a few drops of vanilla extract to the basic fondant mixture.

2 Form into balls about ¾ inch in diameter, then roll in chocolate sprinkles to coat evenly.

• MARASCHINO CREAMS •

1 Add a few drops of Maraschino liqueur and a drop of pink food coloring to the basic fondant mixture.

2 Roll into balls about the size of a cherry. Leave to set on waxed paper.

R·O·S·E C·R·E·A·M·S

MAKES ABOUT ½ lb
5 teaspoons lemon juice
½ teaspoon finely grated lemon rind
4 teaspoons rosehip syrup
A few drops of rose water
Scant 2 cups confectioners' sugar, sieved
Crystallized rose petals, for decoration (page 96)

1 Mix the lemon juice, lemon rind, rosehip syrup and rose water together.
2 Add the confectioners' sugar and work to a stiff mixture using the fingertips.
3 Break off small pieces of the mixture and roll into balls on a work surface lightly dusted with extra sieved confectioners' sugar.
4 Flatten each ball slightly and place a piece of crystallized rose petal on top. Press lightly in place.
5 Place the creams in small paper candy cases and leave in a cool place to dry.

V·I·O·L·E·T C·R·E·A·M·S

MAKES ABOUT ½ lb
A few drops of violet extract
A few drops of violet food coloring
8 oz fondant (any variety)
Crystallized violets, for decoration (page 96)

1 Knead the extract and food coloring into the fondant and leave for 1 hour.
2 Shape into small balls and flatten each one lightly.
3 Place a small piece of crystallized violet in the center of each.
4 Leave to dry for 24 hours.

C·O·C·O·N·U·T A·N·D L·E·M·O·N C·R·E·A·M·S

MAKES ABOUT ¾ lb
Confectioners' sugar, for dusting
A few drops of lemon oil
1⅓ cups shredded coconut
8 oz fondant (any variety)
A few drops of pink food coloring
Superfine sugar, for coating

1 On a surface lightly dusted with confectioners' sugar, knead the lemon oil and coconut into the fondant.
2 Divide the mixture in half and work a little pink food coloring into one half.
3 Using a rolling pin lightly dusted with confectioners' sugar roll each piece into a strip about ¼ inch thick.
4 Place the pink strip on top of the white one and press the two together lightly with a rolling pin.
5 Sprinkle with superfine sugar and leave for 24 hours to dry.
6 Cut into small bars with a sharp knife, and store in a single layer in an airtight container lined with waxed paper, and covered with waxed paper.

• ABOVE •
Rose and Violet Creams
• OPPOSITE •
Coconut and Lemon Creams

F·O·N·D·A·N·T N·U·T·S

Whole nuts
Boiled fondant, flavored and colored if liked,
melted (page 22)

1 Make sure the nuts are completely dry.
2 Lower the nuts individually into the fondant, turn them over so that they are evenly coated, then lift out on a dipping fork or the prongs of an ordinary fork. Tap the fork on the side of the bowl, then draw the underside over the rim of the bowl.
3 Carefully transfer the nuts to waxed paper and leave for about 10 minutes to dry.
4 Place in small paper candy cases.

C·H·O·C·O·L·A·T·E F·O·N·D·A·N·T·S

MAKES ABOUT ¾ lb
⅔ cup semisweet chocolate pieces
Confectioners' sugar, for dusting
8 oz uncooked fondant (page 146)
A few drops of vanilla extract

1 Place the chocolate in a small bowl over a saucepan of hot water, and heat gently until melted.
2 Remove from the heat and allow to cool slightly.
3 Dust a work surface with confectioners' sugar, put the fondant onto the sugar and flatten it out. Make a series of deep slits in the surface.
4 Mix vanilla extract with the chocolate and pour into the slits in the fondant.
5 With hands lightly dusted with confectioners' sugar knead the fondant well to blend the ingredients evenly.
6 Leave for 1 hour.
7 Using a rolling pin lightly dusted with confectioners' sugar, roll the fondant out to about ¾ inch thick. Cut into squares using a sharp knife dusted with confectioners' sugar.
8 Place in small paper candy cases and leave for 24 hours to dry.

D·O·U·B·L·E C·H·O·C·O·L·A·T·E W·H·I·R·L·S

MAKES ABOUT 10 oz
Confectioners' sugar, for dusting
¼ cup white chocolate pieces, finely chopped
8 oz fondant (any variety)
¼ cup semisweet chocolate pieces, finely chopped

1 Lightly dust a work surface with confectioners' sugar.
2 Put the white chocolate into a bowl, place over a saucepan of hot water and heat gently until melted.
3 Remove from the heat and leave to cool slightly.
4 Divide the fondant in half. Put one piece on the confectioners' sugar on the work surface, form it into a ball, then flatten it out. Make a series of slits over the surface.
5 Put the melted white chocolate into the slits, then knead it well to distribute the ingredients evenly.
6 Roll the flavored fondant out to a rectangle using a rolling pin lightly dusted with confectioners' sugar. Trim the edges.
7 Melt the semisweet chocolate and flavor the other piece of fondant in the same way, then roll it out to a similar rectangle.
8 Place the white chocolate fondant on the dark chocolate then roll it up firmly from a long side, like a jelly roll.
9 Cut into slices using a sharp knife lightly dusted with confectioners' sugar.
10 Place in small paper candy cases and leave to dry for 24 hours.

• ABOVE•
Chocolate Fondant (top right)
Fondant Nuts (bottom right)
Double Chocolate Whirls (left)

F·O·N·D·A·N·T F·A·N·C·I·E·S

1 lb FONDANT GIVES ABOUT 20–25 FANCIES
Boiled fondant (page 149)
Flavoring and coloring, to taste
Thin syrup for thinning down (optional)

1 Gently heat some boiled fondant, in a bowl placed over a saucepan of hot water.
If the fondant is plain, flavoring and coloring may be added at this stage.
2 Stir the fondant with a wooden spoon and gradually add a little thin syrup so that the fondant will be just fluid enough to pour when the temperature reaches 140°F. Do not allow the temperature to exceed this figure.
If a liquid flavoring such as a fruit purée or alcohol has been added, it will probably not be necessary to add any syrup.
3 Pour the fondant into small paper candy cases or molds in a rubber fondant mat, or chocolate cases.
4 Place nuts, glacé fruits, crystallized flowers, silver balls etc on the surface to decorate. Leave to cool and set. Store in an airtight container.

F·O·N·D·A·N·T D·I·P·P·E·D F·R·U·I·T·S

½ lb FONDANT FOR ABOUT ¾ lb FRUIT
Small, whole fruit such as strawberries, grapes,
cherries or Cape gooseberries with stems, or perfect
segments of tangerines
Boiled fondant (page 149)

1 Wash small whole fruit, then dry them well.
2 Melt the fondant in a bowl placed over a saucepan of hot water, stirring constantly, and adding a little hot water if necessary if it is too thick, to give an even coating. Do not let the temperature exceed 150°F.
3 Holding each piece of fruit by its stem, or by one end, dip the fruit into the fondant.
4 Allow excess fondant to drain back into the bowl, then carefully lay the fruit on waxed paper and leave to dry for 5–10 minutes.
5 Place in small paper candy cases.

B·O·N·B·O·N·S

Boiled fondant (page 149)
Coloring and flavoring, to taste
Decorations (see below)

1 Form some ripened boiled fondant, flavored and colored if liked, into small balls and leave on waxed paper for 24 hours to dry.
2 Gently heat some more boiled fondant, flavored and colored if liked, in a bowl placed over a saucepan of hot water, stirring with a wooden spoon, until the temperature reaches 140°F. Do not allow it to exceed this figure.
3 Lower the dried fondant balls individually into the coating fondant, turn them over so they are evenly coated, then lift them out with a dipping fork.
4 Tap the fork on the side of the bowl, then draw the underside over the rim. Carefully slip the ball onto waxed paper. Decorate with silver balls, nuts, glacé fruits or small pieces of crystallized flowers, if liked.
5 Leave to dry for about 10 minutes, then carefully place in small paper candy cases.

• ABOVE •
Fondant Dipped Fruits
Fondant Fancies
• OPPOSITE •
Bonbons

• ABOVE •
Coconut Ice
• OPPOSITE •
Sugar Mice

C·O·C·O·N·U·T I·C·E

MAKES ABOUT 1¼ lb
2 cups sugar
⅔ cup milk
1⅔ cups shredded coconut
Red food coloring

1 Oil or butter a pan approximately 8 × 6 inches.
2 Gently heat the sugar in the milk in a heavy saucepan, stirring with a wooden spoon until the sugar has dissolved.
3 Bring to a boil, cover and boil for 3 minutes.
4 Uncover and boil until the temperature reaches 240°F, the soft ball stage.
5 Remove from the heat and stir in the coconut.
6 Quickly pour half of the mixture into the pan.
7 Add a few drops of red food coloring to the remaining mixture and quickly pour it on top of the white mixture.
8 Leave to cool and about half set, then mark into bars or squares with an oiled knife.
9 Leave to set completely, then break or cut into pieces.
10 Wrap in cellophane paper, place in an airtight container and keep in a cool place for up to 7 days.

S·U·G·A·R M·I·C·E

PER MOUSE
2 oz boiled fondant (page 149)
Pink food coloring
2 silver balls
A piece of chocolate button
4–6 bristles from a paintbrush
A piece of white string

1 For white mice, break off about a tenth of the fondant and color it pink. For pink mice, color about nine-tenths pink and leave one-tenth plain.
2 Form the large piece of fondant into a pear shape, then carefully form ears a little way back from the pointed end. Mold the smaller amount of fondant into the inside of the ears.
3 Place silver balls to make eyes, a piece of chocolate button for the end of the nose, and bristles for whiskers. Fix string on the underside of the wide end as a tail.
4 Leave to set.
5 Keep in a single layer in an airtight container lined with waxed paper. The mice should keep for 3 to 4 days if stored in a cool place.

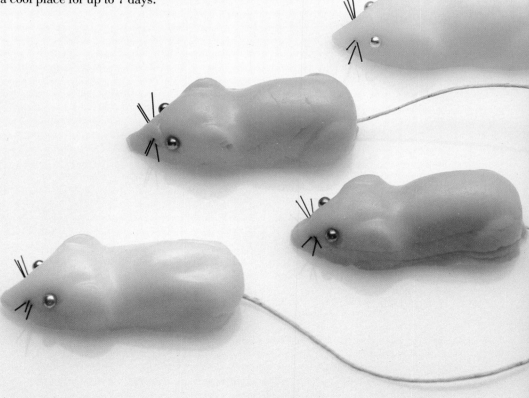

I·N·D·E·X

Page numbers in *italic*
refer to the illustrations.